*To Dear Sr Vincent
with lots of love
& thanks

Mary McD. Garvey*

A TRADITIONAL MUSIC JOURNEY
1600-2000
From Erris to Mullaghban

by
MÁIRE NIC DOMHNAILL GAIRBHÍ

ISBN 1 873437 20 X
The author acknowledges with gratitude the financial assistance of the

The Arts Council
An Chomhairle Ealaíon

Published by
Drumlin Publications
Nure, Manorhamilton, Co.Leitrim, Ireland (072) 55237
E-mail: drumlin@eircom.net
Designed by Daragh Stewart
Printed by Colour Books, Dublin

Acknowledgements

My sincere gratitude to all who encouraged me to carry out the research necessary to compile this collection of music and its history. It has been a very exciting project. My journey from Ceathrú Thaidhg across the counties of Mayo, Sligo, Galway, Roscommon, Leitrim, Fermanagh, Monaghan , Armagh, Louth and Meath to Sliabh Gullion has given me an insight into the life and times of those people who lived two hundred years ago.

My sincere thanks to all my family, Carmel, Ita, Seamus, Sean and Elizabeth who were there when needed, and especially Marie, my daughter who in the midst of her very busy life took the time and care to guide me through the "Dell" and directed me when I went off line. I also wish to thank Gerry, her husband for his patience. Thanks especially to Dónal Ó hEalaí and Ciarán Ó'Raghallaigh, who are both steeped in traditional music, and play all the tunes I have researched. Ciaran notated most of the music. Micháel O' Seighin and his wife Caitlín from Ceathrú Thaidhg, were very helpful with references My thanks to Eamon O'Boyle, photographer whose permission I got to use his photo of Eagle Island, Belmullet.

Dr. Hugh Gibbons of Keadue, played a large part in this research and I thank him sincerely for sharing his knowledge that sunny day last Summer 1999. My friends in Dundalk, Noel McCabe and Catherine Holland were such a great help when we came to South Ulster, Mullaghbán, Forkhill, The Fews, Sliabh Gullion, Ballymascanlon, as we trod the sacred places of the South Ulster Poets. Sincere thanks to Nicholas Carolan of the Irish Traditional Archives (Taisce Cheol Dúchas Éireann) whose advice and comments were invaluable. His encouragement helped me to continue to the end.

My special thanks to all the organisations who were so helpful in every way, The National Library of Ireland, Dublin, including the Prints and Drawing section, The National Gallery, Dublin, Ireland, for permission to publish "Carolan The Harper" by Francis Bindon. Thanks to Ivor Hamroch of the County Mayo library, Castlebar and to Dónal Tinney, chief librarian, County Sligo library and to Helen Kilcoyne, librarian of County Roscommon library. Sincere thanks to the staff in Clondalkin library and the staff of the New Co. Council library in Tallaght, and to Kathy Murphy of the County Council library, Dundalk, Co. Louth.

Thanks to the staff of the Traditional Irish Music Archives, Merrion Square and the staff of the Royal Irish Academy, Dawson Street. Eibhlín Ní Chathailriabhaigh was always there to advise and whose knowledge is invaluable. Many thanks to Séan Ó' Coistealbha, Príomh Óifigeach of Muintearas Co. Mhaigh Eo, and Joe Carey, for their invitation to me on St. Patrick's week, to Teach Iorrais, Co.Mayo to speak on My Traditional Music Journey.

Also I wish to thank John Langton of Tempo, Enniskillen who supplied me with Archival History of the McGuires. I wish to thank also, Crónán Ó'Doibhlin, Archive Co-ordinator of the Cultural Activity Centre, Mullaghbán, Newry, for his important information regarding Ó'Cearbhalláin and the South-East Ulster Poets. I must not forget the Rev. Mervyn Kingston of Lower Faughart, Dundalk, Co. Louth for sending me the video of "Art na gCeoltaí" with the song "Úir Chille Creagain."

I wish to thank Derek O'Brien for his work on the map of the Journey Sincere thanks to Mark and Maeve McLoughlin. Thanks also to Kathy Whereley of the *Western People*, Ballina for the photo of Siobhán McKenna unveiling the plaque on the grave of Riocard Bairéad. I need to thank sincerely Sr. Marie Bernadette of "Caritas" the Sisters of Charity Archives in Sandymount for the research I did on the Jones family of Benada Abbey, Diocese of Achonry. Thanks also to Serena Perceval of Templehouse Co. Sligo and to Madam Felicity Mac Dermot for her very good advice.

I wish also to thank Tom Gaughan and all the staff of his wonderful Teach Iorrais including Deirdre O'Donnell, the artist whose art work is outstanding. The people of Erris are full of warmth, culture and tradition and their welcome was like a breath of fresh air. Special thanks to The Secretary of the Co. Roscommon Council, Derry O'Donnell who initiated the grant from the Roscommon Arts Council.

Thanks to Seán Doherty for his gift and good wishes to, Harry Bradshaw, to Charles Hodgins of Ballymote and to my good friend Libby Walsh. Sincere thanks to all the musicians whose patience I must have tried at times.

CONTENTS

FOREWORD

As the 20th century fades from view, and as a new generation of Irish traditional musicians in their teens and twenties becomes the inheritors of the past, the documenting of that past takes on ever more importance. All the signs are that the future in Ireland will be urban — the countryside has already become suburban. While traditional music will adapt to whatever circumstances come, as it always has, it will lose vitality, depth and meaning if it loses the memory of its rural practice over many millennia and the memory of its life in the cities of Ireland, Britain and America in recent centuries.

Máire Garvey's book contributes to our knowledge of both these areas. A musician, she comes from the countryside near the town of Ballaghaderreen, Co Roscommon, and her earliest memories of traditional music recounted here include women keeners at her grandfather's funeral in 1932, house-dance parties, travelling street pipers and singers, fife and drum bands, the impact of the first commercial recordings that came from America, and the excitement of becoming a sixteen-year-old fiddle player in the local ceili band. She throws light on P.J. Giblin, an almost forgotten traditional composer and collector who published a unique collection of music in 1928 and who was one of her early music teachers. Her book also valuably documents traditional music in Dublin to which she moved in 1948 and where she still lives. The link with the west of Ireland was maintained by attending St Mary's Music Club in Church Street and becoming friends with the many rural musicians who gathered there. The native Dublin musicians also come in for their share of mention among the many musicians named here, as does her active membership of the Walkinstown branch of Comhaltas Ceoltóirí Éireann and the Eamonn Ceannt Ceili Band.

Place and the geography of place is intimately connected with the nature of local tradition, and Máire also documents here, from her reading and from her travels and local researches, the music of the larger musical region into which she was born: that encompassed by the counties of Connacht and south Ulster. Going further back than personal memory can and using published music and song of the past, she wanders in imagination among the region's singers and musicians, poets and patrons, collectors and researchers. Thomas Connellan, Turlough Carolan, Úna Nic Dhiarmada and Tomás Láidir Mac Coisdealbha, Anthony Raftery, Patrick Lynch, and Douglas Hyde are among the many significant figures met with here.

Molaim an dúthracht a léirítear sa leabhar seo, dúthracht don cheol agus don taighde. Dá gcuirfeadh ceoltóirí de ghlúin Mháire tríd an tír a gcuimhní cinn ar phár faoi mar atá déanta aicisean, nach luachmhar an bailiúchán a bheadh againn mar thiomnacht do na glúnta atá le teacht?

Nicholas Carolan
Irish Traditional Music Archive, Dublin

INTRODUCTION

At last I have reached the end of my journey after thinking and dwelling on it for thirty years. I was born in the west of Ireland and came to live in Dublin in 1948. I loved traditional music and our home was always full of players and singers down the years. Coming to live in Dublin was a real culture shock. Coping with this change was not easy until I heard of St. Mary's Traditional Music Club some time later. In time I began research in the National Library on the history of old tunes and all this helped me in running a session in the Belgard Inn, off the Dublin Naas Road, beside Roadstone Castle which was the town House for the Dillons of Loughglynn in the nineteenth century. This session lasted for about nine years. The Belgarde Inn was said to be the largest pub in Europe. I used to play the fiddle reasonably well and loved the excitement of it all.

So last summer I was determined to do this project and connect the tradition in Mayo with South Armagh. It has been the most exciting time of my life. Being from Connacht I realised that this province has always been 'the poor relation' for quite a long time. But in areas you will see on the map there have been hidden cultural activities down through the years in the midst of poverty, hardship, oppression and neglect. Not only in Connacht but right across the country to Sliabh Gullion, Mullaghbán, and across to the Long Woman's Grave in Oriel the traditional music thrived without the help of modern technology. There was an affinity established when the men from The West walked their cattle from Mayo, Roscommon, Sligo and Leitrim across the land of no borders, to load them for export on the cattle boats of Greenore. Those were days of hardship and achievement.

To give you an inkling into the past of three hundred and fifty years ago I present this book with its music, history, hardships, photographs and true stories from Erris in western Mayo, to Galway, Roscommon, Sligo and on to Tempo in Fermanagh and from there to Mullaghbán, Sliabh Gullion and the Fews, Armagh.

Máire Nic Domhnaill, Gairbhí
Máire Mc Donnell Garvey, 2001

TURAS Ó IORRUS GO MULLACH BÁN

Seo achoimre ar an leabhar a scríobhas i mBéarla. Bhí cuid mhaith den Ghaelige ann nuair a bhí mo sheanathair óg. Rugadh é i 1869. Lá amhain nuair a bhí a athair féin agus muinitir na háite ag obair ar an bportach tháinig lead óg, Doubhglas de hÍde trasna na páirce chun caint leo. Is beag Gaeilge a bhí aige an tam sin ach gan dabht d'fhoghlaim sé cuid mhaith uathu.

Nuair a bhí mé féin óg bhí an-chaint ar an veileadóir Mícheál Ó Colmáin agus a dheartháir Jim. Chuaigh Mícheál go dtí na Stáit Aontaithe agus taréis cúpla bliain thosagh céirníní ag teacht amach agus ceol Mhíchíl le cloisteáil orthu. Bhíodh na gramafóin ag seinm ins na siopaí i mBealach a'Doirín gach lá margaidh. Cheannaigh mo mháthair a lán ceirníní mar bhí dúil sa cheol aici.

Ní dhéanfaidh mé dearmad go deo ar an oíche úd sa bhliain 1932 nuair a bhí cóisir i dteach mo sheanathar i gCill Móibhí cúpla míle ó Bhealach a'Doirín. Bhí mo bheirt aintín taréis teacht abhaile ó Mheiriceá chun bualadh lena muinir. Bhí gliondar chroí ar gach duine; bhí an bord lán le bia speisialta agus bhí bairillí de leann dubh ag an gcúl doras. Tháinig ceoltóirí ó gach áit. Bhí an chisitin lán go doras. Lean an chóisir ar feadh na hoíche ar fad. Ón am sin amach lean an grá don cheol tradisiúnta i rith mo shaoil. Cúpla bliain ina dhiadh sin thosaigh mé ag fhoghlaim an veidhlin. PJ Giblin a bhí mar mhúinteoir agam. Tháinig sé ar rothar gach Satharn ó Charlestown. Chuir sé leabhar cheoil i gcló í 1928 ina bhfuil portanna, ríleanna agus cornphíopaí. Bhí mé i mo bhall den bhanna céilí Aiséirí insna daichidí. Bhí sé an spéisiúil ag cleachtadh gach seachtain agus ag seinm ag céilithe ar fud na háite ach nuair a tháinig am na scrúdaithe bhí orm éirí as agus staidéar dian a dhéanamh.

Blianta ina dhiaidh léigh mé scéalta Dhubhglas de hÍde agus na dánta a bhailigh sé. Chuir Dhubhglas agus Éibhlín Bean Uí Choisdealbha leabhair i gló. Tá roinnt mhaith de fhoinn ar an sean nós ins na leabhair sin mar Sail Óg Rua, Peigín Mistéal, Cill Aodáin, Bean an fhir rua, Anach Cuain agus go leor eile.

Amhráin brónach é Anach Cuain a chuirenn síos ar thubaist mhór a thárla ar Loch Coirib I 1828. Bádh naoi nduine déag. Dúirt Rairftéirí nach ndéanfadh sé dearmad go deo ar an lá seo. Fuair de hÍde an chuid is mó de véarsaí an dáin seo ó Phroinnsias Ó Conchubhair. Nuair a bhí mé ag léamh stair chúige Chonnacht chuir mé suim i gceol Uí Chearbhalláin. Rugadh é san Obair i gContae na Mí i 1670 agus mhair sé go 1738. Cláirseoir agus file ba ea é. Bhíodh fáilte roimh na cláirseoirí ins na tithe móra ar fud na tíre. Bhí a lán cairde ag Cearbhallán agus bhí cuid acu ina bpatrúin aige: muinitir Mhic Dhiarmada, muintir Uí Chonchubhair agus muinitir Diolúin mar shampla. Chum sé píosaí ceoil do mhuintir gach tí ar thug sé cuairt air. Cuir i gcás scríobh sé píosa do mhuintir Crofton. Tá stair na clainne seo scríofa agus cuireadh i gcló é i 1911. Thug Ó Cearbhallán cuairt ar Viscount Dillon i gCo Roscomáin agus chum sé amhrán do gach duine sa chlann. Sa cheanntar sin tá ait ar a dtugtar Kingsland. Bhí muintir Drury ina chónaí ann. Daoine mór le rá ba ea iad. Phós duine acu Éilís Goldsmith, colceathar Oliver Goldsmith. Cumadh

Fáilte go Kingsland ina n-onóir. Ó am bás Uí Chearbhalláin is dream beag dícheallach a rinne iarracht ar a chuid ceoil a shábháil.

Caoga bliain ó sin is beag teach san iarthar nach raibh feadóg stáin (Clarke), sean veidhlín nó sean bhosca ceoil crochta suas ar an mballa. Insna tithe is mó a bhíodh an ceol tradisiúnta le cloisteáil. Ní bhíodh morán den cheol insna tábhairní. Bhí rincí agus seisiún ceoil coitianta ag na cros-bhóithre. Bhí an-tóir ar na portanna, The Connacht Man's Rambles agus Farewell to Gurteen an uair sin agus tá siad go mór i mbéal an phobail sa lá atá inniú ann.

Rugadh John Egan I mBaile an Tochair i gContae Shligigh. Nuair a tháinig sé go Baile Átha Cliath chuir sé club beag ar bun do na ceoltóirí tradisiúnta. Gach Céadaoin tháinig siad isteach go dtí an club agus chaith siad an oiche ar fad ag seinm agus ag caint. Bhí an club lonnaithe i Sráid an Teampaill ar dtús. Ansin d'aistrigh sé go Brú na nGael. Taréis tréimhse ansin chuaigh na ceoltóirí go Keoghs i bPáirc an Ghabha, ina dhiaidh sin arís go Sráid Henrietta. Faoi láthair tá an club i Hughes i Sráid Chancery.

Tá píosa scríofa agam faoi Andy Conroy a tháinig ó mo cheantar féin. Fuair sé bás le déanaí agus chuaigh a lán den sean saol san uaigh leis. Fear iontach a bhí ann. Sheinn sé ar an bpíob uilleann. Nuair a bhí sé i mBaile Átha Cliath bhí Leo Rowsome mar theagascóir aige. Chaith sé blianta fada i Sasana.

Tá turas Patrick Lynch ó Béal Féirste go Muigheo an shuimiúl ar fad. Thart faoi 1794 bhí Lynch ina mhuinteoir Ghaeilge sa Belfast agus I dtithe anseo agus ansiúd sa chathar. Ag an am sin bhí na hÉireannaigh Aontaithe gníomhach. Duine acu sin ba ea Tomás Ruiséal agus bhí an suim aige i gcultúr na tíre. Bhí tionchur mór ag Ruiséal ar Patrick Lynch agus thug sé an post dó dul go hIarthar na hÉireann chun na hamhráin ar an sean nós a bhailiú. Tá na litreacha a bhain leis an turas seo i leabharlann Ollscoil na Bainríona I mBéal Feirste. Scríobh Lynch ar na daoine a casadh air, ar na háiteanna éagsúla ar thug sé cuairt orthu agus ar na hamhráin a bhailigh sé. Thug Lynch ard-mholadh do Riocárd Barrett, duine de mhór-fhilí na linne sin. Sa chuid seo den leabhar tá cur síos ar fhilí eile Mhuigheo leithéidí MacSuibhne agus MacCosgair.

Sa chaibidil dheireannach tá cur síos ar chlann Mhic Ghuidhir I gContae Fhearmanach agus ar áiteanna I gContaethe Ard Mhaca agus Lú. Cuirtear síos ar na filí móra, Mac Cuarta, Ó Doirnín, agus Mac Cumhaigh. Tugtar cúntas ar an uair ar bhuail Ó Cearbhallán leo.

From Erris to Tempo to Mullach Bán

CHAPTER 1

MY LIFE IN THE THIRTIES AND FORTIES
MO SCÉAL FÉIN

I grew up in Tobracken, Ballaghaderreen, Co. Roscommon and my love for Irish music goes back to 1932, when Aunt Molly and cousins came home from Providence Rhode Island. There was great welcome for the 'Yanks' as returned Irish were called. There was a special party in the home of my grandfather Talbot in Kilmovee a few miles outside Ballaghaderreen. That night in the ancestral home is clear in my memory. The golden thatched white washed cottage was situated not too far away from the ancient 'Caisiol' of Kilmovee. A thatcher had just finished thatching the roof. Aunt Bea had come home from Manchester for the occasion. Uncle Mike Talbot was very happy with the new suit Aunt Molly had brought him from the U.S.A. Our visitors loved Ireland. Their joy was to breathe the fresh bog air, enjoy the sweet smell of the awakening countryside and breathe in the scent of the new mown hay.

We arrived from Tobracken on the donkey and cart shortly after midday. Even the cradle was taken for my baby brother. The welcome was so good. The hustle and bustle of the preparations left me free to explore the garden where roses and rockets abounded. The house parties were a wonderful source of entertainment during the long winter nights and in summer if an occasional Yank came home. A very important preparation for the night was preparing the lamps, trimming the wicks, and filling the lamp bowls with paraffin. Then the long clear glass globes had to be shone until you could see your reflection in them. I still reflect on the beautiful brass table lamp we had in our house in Tobracken. It was only lit for Christmas and party times. The pink globe cast a rose coloured glow across the room and it was so comforting to sit beside the large turf fire for a few stolen minutes before the musicians arrived. These were the days before we got the electric light. There was always a gross of white candles in each house in case the lamp oil was scarce.

The conversation and excitement in the kitchen preparing for the party that night continued non-stop. Bracks from Monica Duffs and home cooked hams were sliced and the tables were heavy with good things to eat. A barrel of double X porter was rolled in and set up at the end of the kitchen and tapped as soon as the party began. Musicians, young, old, middleaged and ageless took part. Among them were three

Talbot men, cousins of my mother who all played the concert flute very well and a neighbour called Rushe. Jim Talbot, another cousin was quite shy about his music on the flute. When his wife died his son took him to live with him in Mount Charles in Donegal. Some friends and I visited him there and played traditional music for him. He became very emotional, as only the qualities of Irish music are capable of touching one in that way. I felt he was lonesome for the west. He died later that year.

It was the custom at the time for one musician to spread the word about the party and no matter how many came they were all welcome. It was also the custom that the 'musicians' recognised as 'great' were taken to the 'room' first for uisce beatha (generally poitín) and refreshments. They got the pick of the table. Without the musicians it would have been a very poor party. They were treated in the same spirit as the Bards of ancient times. It was a labour of love. The first money paid for music in the west was years later when Céilí Bands began to play in parish halls in the early forties. Younger musicians who sometimes only fingered a tin whistle in the hope of partaking of the 'goodies' had to wait until all the guests had got their share.

As the party in the Talbot household in Kilmovee continued the best of traditional music was played and sparks flew as the tipped boots tapped the flags on the kitchen floor. The dances in those days were the Mazurka, Caledonian sets, half-sets, waltzes, two-steps, highland flings and solo step dancing taught by travelling dancing masters. There has always been speculation as to the origin of dancing in Ireland. The natural expression when listening to good music is to tap your feet or get up and dance.

Once the barrel was tapped there was no stopping the fun. When it was empty there was another one waiting outside the backdoor. There was a feeling of joy and safety in Kilmovee that night that made it never ending. And of course it was the last gathering of those present. We children were allowed to stay up late and had to be coaxed to bed with the bribe of a Clarke's tin whistle under our pillows. We fell asleep to the haunting sounds of traditional music, which has left me with a love for it, something impossible to explain.

Another early memory is now very interesting. There were very few pipers around Ballaghaderreen in the thirties, and mid-forties. I remember a man called Stephen Rainey who played pipes on the street outside Cuniffe's butcher shop on market days. We stood to listen as we were coming home from school and saw passers-by throwing pennies into his cap on the ground beside him. Many people stood to listen. His wife Alice who was a good singer stood by and kept an eye on the money.

At the Féile in Iorras, An tEarrach Thiar on St.Patrick's week-end 2000 I was able to add to my information about the Raineys. Paddy Fitz, who is an outstanding traditional singer, dancer and seanchaí told me the first sight of spring brought wandering minstrels to the towns and villages on fair days, market days, football matches, feiseanna, festivals and carnivals. Paddy remembers the Raineys and took photographs for me of the ruins of the old house where they stayed all winter after travelling from the north.

The Raineys stayed up in Gleantán and as the weather improved went on from there to Caherlestrane the home of the famous traditional singers - The Keane sisters. It was Alice Rainey who gave them the words of those lovely songs they sang down through the years. There were two nephews of Stephen Rainey, who (as Paddy said) lived over in Athenry and they used to come that way when Paddy was a young lad. They were good violin players. They often stayed over in Gleanntán. This is not far from Renvyle.

I remember my father speak of Douglas Hyde's collections of Raftery's airs in Connacht.[1] He said Hyde travelled throughout the province and stayed wherever he could get a bed for the night and wrote down the songs. And of course many of the hard working small farmers thought this was strange behaviour for a minister's son. He also spoke of men cutting turf on the bog at the Float Bridge (between Tibohine and Edmondstown) in my grandfather's time. While sitting around a lit fire where they had boiled the kettle for tea, Hyde, a young lad of fourteen or so would join them and try to take part in the conversation.

Photograph of Roscommon men after Mass.

In the photograph above there are no ladies present. So I presume they were considered unimportant! The man seated in the centre, Mr. Tully from Newtown Athlone, was the father of ten children and his eldest daughter Nellie had to look after each one in turn. She was so weary of this that she left for England during the First World War, and got a job as a bus conductor. The week the war was over she got notification from the Government Department of Transport, stating that her employment was being terminated as the men coming back from the war needed the jobs. She was furious as she had worked hard those years and finished up with an official piece of paper stating her services were no longer needed. She then went to the States where she worked very hard. She never married. She was a strong independent woman.[2]

Roscommon men on a bog in 1870.

This photograph was taken on a bog in Co. Roscommon in 1870.[3] The family, men, women, children and even the dogs all came together at lunchtime. When the fire was built, the kettle boiled and the tea made they sat around and ate heartily of the food the women had provided. There was tasty freshly made oven baked bread and lashings of thick home cooked ham. It has been said that no tea was ever as tasty. And then one of the younger lads was sent to the nearest "local" (maybe a mile away) for a crock of "Double X". They brought fresh buttermilk to the bog with them and put the bottles into the bog hole, to keep it cool for the thirst. Often the conversation turned to songs, history and tunes. The men debated the state of the country and the hardships that were being endured. Their language was Irish. Is it any wonder the young Douglas Hyde wanted to learn Gaeilge?

There was great talk of the fiddler Michael Coleman and his wonderful music. My mother bought every record of his that came on the market, in Tim Kenny's shop in Ballaghaderreen.[4] Owen Coleman, Michael's grandfather was a native of Banada outside Ballaghaderreen on the road to Dublin. My step grandmother was Coleman from Banada and I remember a Fr. Coleman coming home from Rhode Island and visiting the Banada Colemans and saying there was a relationship there. Tim Kenny's hardware shop was a gold mine of music each market and fair day. The gramophones and seventy-eight records blazed out, playing records of Michael Coleman, Paddy Killoran, James Morrison and many more. Paddy Mulligan was in charge of the hardware. It was in the early forties the records came on sale. A friend of ours, John Murray, asked Paddy how much was Michael Coleman's record. Two and six pence he said. John put his hand in his pocket and all he had was two shillings. 'That is all right' says Paddy. 'Take the record and you can pay me next week'. John still talks of that day and the kindness of Paddy Mulligan. The craze for traditional music was so great in those years that there was no danger it would ever die out. It was in 1921 Michael Coleman made his first recording.[5] We listened in ecstasy to these records until we got the tunes in our heads and long afterwards were able to transfer them to our fingers.

Owen Coleman's family were all born at Killavil, Co. Sligo. A brother of Michael's, Jim, married Maenie Dyer and they lived in a tiny house with a half door in Drumacoo. Jim's fiddle playing was delightful but there was no chance of making recordings at that time in Ireland. Michael's records are still the most popular in traditional circles. Styles of fiddle playing differed from county to county but players could meet from the four corners of Ireland and play the same tunes. They seemed to complement one another.

I have always felt that the local history of all tunes is very important. It gives body to the music and we can rejoice or mourn for those whom the music is built around. In 1893 when the Gaelic League was formed people became aware that knowledge of the language was very important to collectors of our music. 'Sean-Nós' singing is generally unaccompanied.

There has been a major loss throughout the country of music and songs due to the changeover from Irish to English. But we still have enough to be proud of. Reels and jigs are played mostly at sessions but when a sweet traditional air is played on a concert flute one can hear a pin drop. We do not hear enough airs. Brendan Breathnach said that a sean-nós singer never sings any two verses of a song in the same way but the variations must not interfere with the basic structure of the song.[6]

When I was eleven years old I had the good luck to have an excellent teacher of the violin. He was a Mr. P.J.Giblin from Charlestown and he cycled the 10 miles to Ballaghaderreen very week. Seemingly he was born in Castlerea years before and emigrated to England. He studied and could play many instruments. He published his collection in 1928.[7] It is called

COLLECTION OF TRADITIONAL IRISH DANCE MUSIC FOR THE VIOLIN
Also
21 ORIGINAL COMPOSITIONS FOR PIANO OR VIOLIN
Composed and arranged by P.J.Giblin.
Price 3/6

It was printed in Germany and had international copyright and copyright in the U.S.A in 1928. He was living in Castlerea when this was published. He states in the preface that he wishes to thank Mr. Arthur Darley for his valuable assistance and advice as he says his sympathy with the promotion and fostering of Irish music is known wherever Irish music is played. Mr. Darley writes " I like your book of Dance Tunes greatly, also your bowing and editing. I think it will be a valuable addition to Irish dance music. You deserve to be congratulated for your splendid work in editing these dance tunes in such an excellent manner".

Brother Cassian Kelly set up a fife and drum band for boys when I was twelve years old. This band played at processions, outings, masses and celebrations. They had a good friend in Mr. Deely who was the band master and he conducted and cared for about fifty boys at each performance. Years later they entered for all the Fleadhanna Ceoil in Connacht and invariably won. Matt Molloy of the Chieftains was a member of this band.

I had been learning the piano from a music teacher in the town called Chrissy (Christine) Keenan. We had no piano at home. But some years before, my mother had bought a violin from an uncle who wanted to return to New York. He was short of money so he sold his violin to her for £15. Thinking it all out my mother paid a visit to Brother Cassian and said she was interested in my learning the fiddle from Mr. Giblin. He was doubtful as no girl had ever set foot in the De La Salle School since it was built. Later he said that if there were two more girls he would agree. Eventually quite a few girls agreed to join the class, Tilly Coleman and Vera McGovern just to mention two. We had broken the mould. The boys school would never be out of bounds again. Brother Cassian Kelly was director of the Institute of the Brothers of the Christian Schools in Ballaghaderreen in 1936.[8] They were called the De La Salle Brothers after their founder John Baptist de La Salle who set up the order in 1851. They had set up a school in Ballaghaderreen in 1890.

So every Saturday morning I set out on my bicycle carrying my fiddle case. For the first few weeks my friends jeered me but they got tired. Mr. Giblin was an excellent teacher and very exact. I spent three years going to that school. In 1940 my mother sent to Pigott & Co. Ltd., Grafton St. for a copy of Captain O'Neills "1001 Dance Tunes of Ireland". I still have the violin and the music book as well as Mr. Giblin's book. While his health permitted Mr Giblin attended all the functions and they were always a great success. He died some years ago at a great age.

ESTERSNOWE

The ancient name for this beautiful air is known as Diseart Nuadhain. This has been mentioned in the Annals of the Four Masters, which was compiled, 1632-36. Estersnowe is situated four miles outside Boyle in Co. Roscommon as you go towards Croghan.[10] The name suggests a place of retreat. In the barony of Boyle, Co. Roscommon there is a parish called Estersnowe. In the parish there are 23 townlands and one of them is named Estersnowe. Here on the borders of that small townland is the ancient graveyard of Ardcarne. The remains of an old Abbey or Hermitage is in the graveyard itself and has been restored for the Millenium and old headstones have the name of the townland - Estersnowe carved on them. George Petrie (1789-1886) collected 1,528 traditional tunes while travelling throughout Ireland for the Ordinance Survey mapping section in Phoenix Park. This air is part of that collection, number 1123. We do not know who composed it but it is certainly one of Ireland's best.

Many people have written about Estersnowe. Seán O'Boyle from Northern Ireland said in 1965 that this is a love song of the *pastourelle* type. As a result of the suppression of the Irish language English words were put to the air. The young lady in the song is a symbol of Ireland. Perhaps the last two lines of the air proves this.

My heart is not my own to give, nor can I it bestow.
'Tis pledged to one who lives and loves far from Estersnowe'.

Sam Henry in his 'Songs of the People' in 1925, calls it Wester Snow. He said the words are difficult to adapt to the air and should be sung by a traditional singer. Sean O'Boyle also got this air from Brigid Tunney, in Belleek, Co. Fermanagh. It was a great favourite of Séamus Ennis. It is a pity Mr. Giblin did not write about the air he loved so well.

Growing up in the west of Ireland I heard men going to the creamery lilting airs as they jogged along in their long carts. Women sang in the fields while saving the hay. Children played rounders to a local ditty. Both men and women hummed or sang to the cows as they milked them. Not many of us had a very learned knowledge of music but we all loved it. House dances were normal every winter. Older men and women sang songs of all kind. Unfortunately for generations before this, our Irish culture had being pushed to the barren regions of the west. But we were so steeped in tradition we never lost our love of it.

Traditional music was spoken of as anonymous as it has passed on from generation to generation. When we hear people say "this is Coleman's reel or McKenna's Jig or Morrison's or Paddy Killoran's hornpipe" we become aware that it is a heritage that had passed from one century to the next, and no one knows who composed the tunes. But they nearly always ended up being called by the name of the person who played them most.

There was scarcely a house in the west of Ireland that did not have a Clarke's tin whistle, a fiddle or an old melodeon at the beginning of this century. The fiddle generally hung on the wall beside the fire (without a case). The whistle or melodeon took pride of place on the high mantelpiece. I am speaking of the thirties and forties. There were no concerts in halls, no groups in public houses and no competitions in local areas to see who was the better player only Feiseanna run by Connradh na Gaeilge. The excitement of having a session, a get together or a céilí in the village was an incentive to do double the work you had to do that day.

In summer time and autumn, crossroad dancing was looked forward to. It was a great time to be alive. It was a happy, carefree interesting decade. There was no television to let us see the atrocities going on in Germany. We were very far removed from the cruel war in Europe. The voice of Lord Haw Haw, (Joyce) during the Second World War, on the Wireless (as the Radio was called then) saying - "Germany calling, Germany calling, " was never frightening as he invariably mentioned the Gurteen pub - Sailor Jordans, saying he would soon call again. There was no fear listening to him. Sailor Jordans was always a good place for music and conversation. But as children we were never allowed into public houses. Seán Donegan took over that pub later and the music flows there to this day.

Often when a ball alley was not being used the musicians and dancers arrived on a Sunday afternoon and danced to their heart's content to our reels, jigs, hornpipes and polkas. Or after an election when the celebrations were high, people gathered on local bridges and danced and sang until the early hours of the morning. I can well remember when Clann na Talún (The Farmers Party) did well in the election we had a wonderful night on Tonroe Bridge which was on the Edmondstown Road going to Sligo. There were very few motor cars then. The dancers moved to one side to let the motor through and then continued on with the dancing.

In winter a granary was an ideal place to hold a céilí. This was a two-storey out-house used for housing cattle underneath and generally for storing grain on the second floor when the threshing was finished. So there was plenty of use made of it until the grain was ready to be stored, generally around October. There was always a stone stairs on the outside leading to the granary which was as clean as a new pin.

*My Grandparents **Patrick & Ellen Talbot***

Another memory of the late thirties was of an old itinerant fiddler who called to our house every time he passed that way. He brought his two little grand-sons with him. My mother made tea for them and he asked about the fiddle. She handed it to him and he played the most beautiful Irish music. The memory of that music always remained with me. He told my mother that it was a very good fiddle but that it needed to be played often. So my mother lent it to my uncle and he played it until I started to learn from Mr. Giblin.

In the mid-forties I was still playing the fiddle. My uncle Mike Talbot who played fiddle and flute was a member of a local céilí band. Pat Casey was the leader and his son Oliver played the piano accordion, Joe Keenan on the drums, Joe Giblin on the fiddle, an excellent player, and his cousin John Drury played the concert flute, and Patsy Mc Hugh played the accordion. In the late 1930s Pat Casey and Mike Talbot played in Clogher Hall at Céilí's mostly for Lancers and old Time Waltzes. (They got £2 per night).

In 1938 Pat purchased a piano accordion for Oliver and the little band grew big-ger and bigger. Then Pat and Oliver bought a set of drums. The music was well improved. However when they got an engagement in Ballaghaderreen Fr. Roughneen refused to allow the drums to be used. Pat Casey was furious and gave notice that weekend. The church was in charge of the halls. It was 1943. Only when Fr. Roughneen was transferred did the band go back to Clogher Hall again. Why some of the clergy had an objection to drums never fails to amaze me.

At that same time the older men in the townland of Tobracken played music up and down the area on New Year's Eve. The drums were kept in our house in a spare room upstairs. Old Davy Morrisroe played the Big Drum and there was always competition as to who would play the kettle drums. When they had finished their round and the drums were in safe keeping again, they all adjourned to the local pub of Tommy Phillips. Then one day Fr. Roughneen sent some men to our door to collect the drums. My mother handed them over and that was the last time they were seen again. There was never an explanation given. An article by Fintan Lane in the Journal of the Irish Labour History Society, Saothar 24, *Music and violence in Working Class Cork: the 'Band Nuisance', 1879-82* throws some light on the origins of this clerical opposition.

At the end of the nineteenth century, street disorders, brass bands and political unrest had their origins in political and religious divisions. There were riots in Dublin and throughout the country sometimes causing loss of life. Bands played at weddings and marched through the streets of the cities or through the small villages. They often played late into the night and the 'Church' said that any girl who followed them had lost all sense of shame and decency. In 1879, the police claimed that women behaved much worse than the men. The disturbances most recorded were in Cork where the *Cork Daily Herald* and the *Cork Examiner* reported them consistently 1870-1882. Tension grew rapidly. The big drum was considered almost a totem pole by the fife and drum bands. Police were called in to disperse the crowds. On one occasion three priests from the Catholic church made an unsuccessful attempt to disperse the rioters. At Mass the following Sunday one of the priests said 'it was the first time that the advice and authority of the clergy was disregarded'

So ' the land war' of 1879-82, was not confined to rural Ireland. The Land League 1879 provided a voice for troubled tenant farmers. The musical bands were not actively involved but allied to the aggressive land agitation in rural Ireland they brought a great deal of civil unrest. Clergy and police were unsuccessful in quelling this state of affairs. In 1880 a Catholic priest asked his congregation to stop this 'band nuisance'. The clergy and the magistrates eventually checked them.

I would safely say the reason the clergy in the west of Ireland were against bands and drums in the forties was a continuation of the fear of the repetition of the 'band violence'. On the other hand I cannot recall any violence when De Valera came to a political meeting in Ballaghaderreen, in the late thirties, when marching bands converged on the town from every road.

In the mid-nineteen forties a political movement was started in Dublin by An tUasal Ó'Cuineagáin. It was very much alive in the west and when there were any functions Pat Casey's "The Aiséirí Céilí Band" got the work. By this time at the age of sixteen in 1943 I was a member of the band. We played in Ballaghaderreen, in Lisacul, in Loughglynn, in Charlestown, in Corrigans Hall, in Carrycastle and in Ballyhaunis and in a hall called Molly the Bogs. This was only a few miles from Ballyhaunis on a sharp turn on the edge of the bog. My mother said it was only because my uncle was a member of the band that she gave me permission to play with them.

We went to all those halls on our bicycles, carrying our instruments on the handlebars. There was a very steep hill leading to Corrigan's hall and the climb was an effort. Some of us walked but there was a very funny incident when Joe Keenan was near the top of the hill with the drums on his back he slipped back. No one could help him. Luckily he was all right but we could not stop laughing. The next engagement was in Ballyhaunis. We hired a car for that. It is about seventeen miles away. The music was great and of course we practised in each other's houses every week. Then when exam time was near I had to stop playing in the band and do extra study.

One afternoon we played at the ball alley in Drumacoo. What a time! People came from all parishes around. Dancers whirled around with fast steps, and sparks were raised from the floor. Anyone who had an instrument was asked to join in. The excitement was high and the music was great. The following Sunday we entered the band at a Féis in Boyle. We got first prize and part of it was to play for the céilí in St. Patrick's Hall that night. My mother had come with us and she was so pleased. She encouraged musicians at all times. On winter nights we had many dances at home and on one occasion twelve of the best musicians from the parish played the greatest music ever. So it is easy to see how I missed the greatest part of my life - music, when I came to Dublin in 1948.

My journey back to the west of Ireland each year, kept my incentive for music and tradition alive. I brought my fiddle with me to Dublin and the only opportunity I had to play was at the children's birthdays. Then in the mid-fifties a friend invited me to her home to a party. It was a wonderful night of traditional music. The following week we went to a music club in Church Street. At last I began to feel at home in Dublin. But I still continued my journeys to the west. There was a hunger in me to learn more about the tunes and the people for whom they were composed. Going back so often, inspired me to write this book.

There are so many musicians I could mention in the west. One of these is Willie Coleman, a fiddler from Carnaree outside Ballymote Co. Sligo. Musicians came from all over the country to see him and he had an open house for all. He was a neighbour of Dan Healy and they had played together in the Glenview céilí band. Willie died in 1983 and was mourned by all. Three years later I was in the west and went to the unveiling of a plaque to his memory. It had been made by Jimmy Joe McKiernan who was a good stone mason but also a good fiddler. It was erected in the front wall of Willie's house. People came from far and near and there were competitions after the unveiling. A large lorry was decorated for this. In the midst of all the hilarity I was invited to adjudicate the adult Fiddle competition. I declined but J.J. McKiernan was very persuasive. I felt so incompetent.

There were only three competitors, Fred Finn, and Tommy Flynn, both deceased, and Peter Horan. These people were legends and I had always admired their music. I was as the saying goes 'tré na chéile'. But I gave the appearance of being cool.

I listened carefully to each man play a jig, a reel and a slow air. Praying and playing for time I asked each one to play three different tunes each. They were all so tense as if their lives depended on this. With inspiration from above I stood up and gave my verdict.

I said each of them had a distinctive style of his own and had proved over the years how excellent they were. Then I said I firmly believed that competitions were solely for those up to eighteen years of age. Then I continued " For adults there should only be exhibitions". The cup was then to be held by each man for four months. The late Fred Finn got the cup for the first four months and he died before the year was out. It was 1986. All agreed it was a great idea and the dancing and sessions went on all evening.

Right to left - Front row: **Seán Garvey, Padráic Walsh, Terence Woodhead, Colm Carroll.**
Second row: **Maura Reck, Jim Carroll, Robert Agnew, Noel and Gerard Carroll.**
Back row: **Una Reck, Marie Garvey and Pat Carroll.** (1964) [9]

Meanwhile Comhaltas Ceoltóirí Éireann had been founded in Dublin for musicians. At the first meeting of the Dublin County Board I was appointed secretary. Micheál Ó h-Aluinn had recently resigned to further his studies. He now teaches on Iniseer. We had an excellent branch in Walkinstown. We had rented a small hall on Crumlin Road and met there once each week. My husband encouraged about twenty-five young-sters to learn the accordion and he made the garage habitable. Alan Begley came out from Parliament Street to teach them. From that we had dancing classes and then Joe Lynch came out from Pigotts to teach the drums. This activity opened up new visions for the children who really came to appreciate Irish Music.

They played at parties for Old Folk, at concerts in the Clarence Hotel and in Moran's Hotel. And when they got their photos in the papers there was no stopping them. Of all the students only Seán, my son, and Padraic Walsh continued to play in later life. The Carroll brothers attended the School of Music in Chatham Row, and they played for many years for tourists in Jury's Hotel. When all was going very well we got a letter from Comhaltas headquarters, requesting us to turn over any assets we had to them and asking for whatever instruments were not being used. I can still get annoyed when I think if it. We held a meeting and resigned from Comhaltas as a branch. They had never helped us out in any way. No one was interested in money in those days except Comhaltas.

CHAPTER 2

MUSIC FORBIDDEN AND PARDONS GIVEN

We should be happy that no one is being penalised today for playing Irish music! Playing music is a time of joy and happiness. But this was not true of the earlier centuries. Grattan Flood who wrote *The Story of the Bagpipe* makes it clear that pipers were outlawed as a class and imprisoned in times of trouble. The first enactment against "Rymoures, Bardes, and dice players" was on December 20th 1563. War pipers made incursions into the Pale and those accused were outlawed and sometimes transported to the West Indies.[1] Occasionally, through the intercession of 'friends in high places' pipers were pardoned. Quite a few of them came from Mayo, Roscommon, Sligo, Leitrim, Cavan and Monaghan.

Bagpipes are associated with ancient Ireland and are mentioned in the 5th century Brehon Laws. Professor O'Curry tells us of this in his *Manners and Customs of the Ancient Irish* that the development and specialisation of music was of very ancient origin. It existed long before the arrival of the Milesians. Daghda, the great chief of the Druid of the Tuatha De Danann, played the three musical feats which gave distinction to a harper: the Suantraighe, (which caused sleep,) the Geantraighe (which caused merriment and laughter), and the Goltraighe, (which caused crying).

The Fomorians, one of the six pre-christian peoples who tried to colonise Ireland had carried off Uaithne, and his harp. Dagda played these pieces when the harper was found. This may be legend and there is good reason to believe that these fabulous stories have been handed down by word of mouth by many generations and eventually were committed to writing. The legends relate how five successive colonies settled in Ireland many centuries before the Christian era.[2]

The first colony was the Parthalonians, who came from Greece. The second, were the Nemedians who came from Scythia. The third colony was the Firbolgs and their dwellings are still on the summit of Carrowkeel in Co. Sligo. These are identical with the tombs at Newgrange and perhaps when they are explored we may find more answers. Not since 1911 has there been any excavations carried out. The fourth colony was the Dedannans who lived at Athens in Greece for many generations. The fifth were the Milesians from Spain.[3]

These peoples, being of ancient origin must have had the basic threads of traditional music in their genes, not the tradition as we know it today, but the combined flow of Grecian, Spanish and Mediterranean music which became part of our heritage before the dawn of history. There must have been a fusion of culture between the invaders and the native population. From the earliest times the Irish were celebrated for their skill in music. Irish professors and teachers of music were sought for abroad. In the seventh century Gertrude the abbess of Nivelle in Belgium, engaged Follian and Ultan, brothers of the Irish saint Fursa to teach her nuns the psalms.[4]

Geraldus Cambrensis (the Norman Gerald Fitzgerald) Archdeacon of St. David's who came to Ireland in 1183, had nothing good to say about the Irish in the twelfth century except this, speaking of Harpers: "They are incomparably more skilful than any other nation I have ever seen. It is astonishing that in so complex and rapid a move-ment of the fingers the musical proportions, as to time, can be preserved; and that the harmony is completed with such sweet rapidity".[5]

Bagpipes were always played at religious services in early Christian times. No important funeral took place unless headed by a band of warpipes. Gradually the Union pipes or Uilleann pipes superseded war pipes. Grattan Flood says that the last historic mention of Irish warpipes was at the Battle of Fontenoy in 1745. The Irish Brigades in the service of France turned the tide in the battle against the English troops.

Joseph Cooper Walker says: 'the character of the bard once so reverenced in Ireland began to sink into contempt in the reign of Queen Elizabeth.' Grattan Flood's research brought to light the names of harpers and pipers who had been forgotten. In the Calendar of State papers there is some information about these musicians who got state pardons. In a proclamation issued on January 28th 1603, Queen Elizabeth gave orders to Lord Barrymore "to hang harpers, wherever found, and destroy their instruments." Later she pardoned one piper and two harpers.

It is interesting to find so many pardons in the west of Ireland.[6] In 1603, two Ballymote harpers Owen O'Mowrigan and Masellong O'Daly were pardoned as well as a piper called Bryan Boy O'Clabby. This information is all the more important as we had no idea of a tradition of pipers or harpers in Ballymote or Achonry. Four harpers in Achonry were pardoned, Gillepatrick O'Finane, Shane Boy O'Finane, Edmund Óg O'Finane and Brian Doerough O'Finane. These were probably all of the one family. Then in Moygara in the half barony of Coolavin two harpers were pardoned, Irriel McDonnell Keogh O'Higgins and Owen O'Higgins. Poets in those days were called rhymers. Fearfassa O'Duignenan of Moygara was a rhymer. There were six rhymers in the Ballymote area, Gillepatrick Cam McEdward, Donald McEdward, Geoffrey McEdward, Twohall Ó'Higgin, Cormac O'Higgin and Taig Mc Teig Dall Ó'Higgin.

In the reign of Elizabeth and James 1, there were pardons and grants in the barony of Corran and Tirrerill Co. Sligo. [7] In the time of Cromwell, Cornelius O'Brien, a piper, was sentenced to twenty lashes to his bare back and transportation to the Barbados. Many of his friends had been sent there before him. Many pipers were punished for "piping before a corpse going to church".

Irish pipers existed in large numbers in England around the mid-nineteenth century. Michael Gaynor and Michael Carolan were both pipers from Louth. Michael Carolan, born in 1810, lived in New York and learned the art of pipe making in his youth. He was one of the few musicians who could read music. He played in the staccato style. He died in 1894.

John McDonogh was born in the parish of Annaghdown on the shores of Lough Corrib in Co. Galway and was known to be an excellent piper. He was known as Mac an Asal as his father was a dealer in asses. He made a practice of making young Johnny pipe him along the road to fairs and markets while he was mounted on a donkey. He was known in later years as 'Home with the rent' from one of his favourite expressions. He travelled Ireland and in Dublin he played on the streets and on the bridges over the Liffey. The audience loved his playing and often the gentlemen carried him to clubs to play. He was often intoxicated when he returned to play for the street audiences and many of them stoned the clubs and broke windows. After the famine years many people were crushed by poverty and Johnny went back to Annaghdown. He died of neglect in Gort workhouse in 1857. His pipes were sold for a trifle. His widow sold them to a Dublin pipe maker. One of his daughters Mrs Kenny was known as "The Queen of Irish Fiddlers".[8]

Gusty Nichols was piper to a gentleman in Cavan for ten years and was part of his household. He was given fifty pounds per annum and the use of a horse. He was always restless with the first touch of spring and often ran away with the first batch of tinkers or nomads for the summer and returned in winter. Edward Blake was a gentleman piper from Castleblake near Tuam. He was the ancestor of Edward Blake MP. for Longford in the mid-nineteenth century. In the *Freeman's Journal*, September 1811, it is noted that Jeremiah Murphy from Loughrea was a famous piper.

Patrick Walsh of Mayo went to England and when he returned in the mid-nineteenth century he settled in Swineford and taught music. In 1823, Jimmy O'Brien of Swineford was the blind pupil of the Walsh brothers of Ballina. Augustus Nicolls a local landlord in the barony of Carrigallen, Co. Leitrim, an excellent performer on the pipes, taught his cousin the Rev. Alexander Nicholls to play. Alexander had a complete aversion to women and when the lady who was responsible for his being made a Minister of the Established Church failed to secure him as a husband for her sister she had him transferred to the poorer parish of Kilgariff. He continued to play his bagpipes in solitude and no woman was permitted to invade his privacy.

Colonel Francis Nesbit of Derrycarn in north east Roscommon not far from Drumod sold his estate to an Englishman at an auction. The new owner, a devotee of pipe music, gave a barbecue to his new tenants at which thirty pipers attended. From this number the new landlord selected nine of the best performers to compete for prizes. Owney Brennan was proclaimed the champion and his rendering of "Lady Kelly's Reel" was regarded as outstanding. One of the Galway Joyces got second prize and the third went to a piper in Drogheda. In researching this I found it difficult to find the reel anywhere. Eventually I went to the Traditional Music Archives in Merrion Square and found it there.[9]

Lady Kelly's Reel
(or Up Roscommon!)
As played by John Kelly of San Francisco

This famous reel as played by John Kelly a fiddler of phenomenal execution now living in San Francisco Cal. is a florid setting of Sergt. James O'Neill's "Northern Lasses" printed in the O'Neill Collections Kelly a native of Roscommon, Ireland, says this reel was known as "Kelly's Reel" before his time.
It was his masterly rendering of "Lady Kelly's Reel" that won the championship for Owen Brennan an expert piper, as described on page 215. *Irish Minstrels and Musicians*.

Owney Brennan had the reputation of being a 'character'. He rode around in his donkey and cart playing the pipes. When any of his friends or acquaintances were leaving for America it was his custom to accompany them from their home to the town of Longford, and from there to where the Royal Canal reached the river Shannon. Here they boarded a boat and continued their journey. An unusual man, he was a great favourite. He was neither lame nor blind, as many of the pipers of that time were. He took to being an itinerant musician because he wanted to.

Another piper born in 1815, was Michael Wallace of Doolagh, Belmullet. His father had married Cecilia Dooyork and they had two sons, Michael and Francis. Both were expert pipers but it was said Michael was the better. On their mother's side all her brothers were good performers on flute, fiddle and pipes. Their father died while they were very young and they were brought up in the home of a maternal uncle. Michael joined the army while still a young man. On the completion of his service he returned to Belmullet.

It was only when he entered for the Feis Ceoil that it was clear that Michael was by far the superior of his contemporaries.[10] Captain O'Neill in his *Irish Minstrels and Minstrelsy* says " This most celebrated of two brothers rivalled the renowned William Connolly on the Uilleann pipes." Michael Egan the famous Dublin piper and pipemaker and a competent judge, awarded him the palm of superiority as an Irish piper on both sides of the Atlantic. He must have had a great gift because when he was in the army the Colonel of the regiment heard Michael's playing and asked him to entertain his fellow officers with some music. Michael agreed but as he had no pipes the Colonel lent him his. When the guests had left the Colonel said "I see you can do justice to that set of pipes. I cannot. They should be in the hands of one who knows so well how to use them. Wallace if you consent to accept them, I make you a present of them." The pipes were accepted and it was with them he afterwards delighted numerous audiences.

For many years Wallace played at weddings, dinner parties and social gatherings in and around Belmullet. On leaving the Church after a wedding the couple were met at the door by Michael who to the strains of "Haste to the Wedding" conducted them to a restaurant for light refreshments before returning home. The shrill notes of the war pipes brought many faces to the windows and doors to see what the excitement was all about. Michael also played jigs, reels and the rince fada for step dancers.

As different instruments were introduced in the area and his profession declined he left his home for Ballinasloe where he spent the remainder of his life. When he knew he was about to die he bequeathed all he valued most in the world, his pipes, to his old friend Denis Delaney. He died on the 22nd November 1898, aged 83 years. It was Delaney who saw to his burial and had him placed in the enclosure that contained the remains of Denis's parents in the old cemetery, Church St., Ballinasloe, Co. Galway. Flaitheas Dé le anam na marbh. Wallace was a fluent Irish speaker.

Denis Delaney was a native of Ballinasloe. Though totally blind he was gifted with great conversational powers, and as a prize-winning piper he won the hearts of every gathering. He never boasted about what he had done for his friend Wallace. But all knew he had "come in" for this beautiful set of pipes and he took no time in selling his own which had been made by the celebrated elder McKenna (one of the famous Dublin pipemakers) in 1781. As a prize winner at pipers' competitions all over Ireland he had no equal. He received 29 firsts, 12 seconds, and 6 third places. It was a deep sadness to his self-esteem when, with the passing of time the adjudicators awarded prizes to others at the Feis Ceoil from 1912.

In her *Annals of the Irish Harpers*, Charlotte Milligan Fox speaks of two rare types of verse adopted by country people on the banks of the river Bann. From the opposite sides of the water they taunted and hailed each other in song.

> Make my respects to that young man
> That has got on the coat of green
> Ask him, does he remember the day
> When the wind did blow my hat in the Bann?
> Um-m-m-m

A humming chorus, called a Crónán followed here, instead of the too mournful "Ochone", then another verse. Charlotte says she cannot say if the custom of singing across the Bann was still prevalent in her time or not. Another verse after the Crónán went like this.

> "Make my respects to that young man
> That has got on the coat of brown;
> It was not the coat I valued a farthing,
> But the ribband my true love put on."
> (Crónán here Um-m-m-m.)

The fact that it is called a Crónán is of interest, as the humming of a bass to a melody is one of the lost arts of Irish music.[11] Lady Morgan says in her Memoirs that her father hummed a crónán just before he died in 1806.

Fr. Peadar Ó'Laoghaire had an interesting few words to say about the Crónán. At the end of the 1870s or thereabouts, every baby in a cradle in Ireland had a Crónán hummed to him every night before going to sleep. Today we would call this a lullaby. He claims that as long as a Crónán was hummed or sung to babies from their birth the Gaelic language was ingrained in each child and that child never lost that first language. [12]

"Siád mar a chuirfinn-se mo leanbh a chodla;
Seo-ín seó,bhú leó leó;
I mbár na gcraobh, 's an ghaoth 'ghá bhogadh.
Seo-ín seó. Bhuú leó, leó"

But then he said, a great change came. The women got interested in the English language and cast aside the sweet musical Crónán that they had learned from their mothers.

CHAPTER 3

FORGOTTEN WOMEN OF IRELAND

From the earliest centuries the women of Ireland played an important role in the life of the country. During the time of the Brehon laws they held a very strong position. On the abolition of the Order of the Bards, the business of lamenting the dead or as we know it the "caoining of the dead" was carried out by a certain number of mercenary women mourners. Up to this time pipers and harpers (all men) led the funerals to the grave and played mournful dirges for the deceased. The women attended the funeral, dressed sometimes in white and sometimes in black as they walked slowly after the hearse, singing extempore odes in which they praised all the virtues of the desceased. The Venerable Charles O'Conor spoke of it in his day as being so remote from the original and as being a barbarous but innocent custom.[1] The caoin or howl was a wild melancholy sound which portrayed real sorrow in the people.

In 1932 my grandfather died in his small native village of Ardvarna outside Ballaghaderreen. Three women (ageless) in black shawls on their heads 'caoined 'at the bedside. There was a wake all night long, as was the custom in the country. Neighbours called throughout the night. My grandfather James Talbot was laid out on the bed with hands joined and dressed in a brown habit with symbols of Christ on the cross on the front. There were lighted candles on a small table at the head of the bed. Holy water in glass dishes were in front of the candles. As people came to pay their respects they shook some holy water on the corpse and then sat along the wall. Left on the body of the corpse was a plate of tobacco, clay pipes and cigarettes and all were welcome to partake.

The rosary was recited a few times during the night. But what the men liked best was the crocks of porter. As each one partook of the drink the stories began to flow of old bygone days. And there was music played. There were ten or more of us children and in the morning we were sent off to the well garden to play until it was time for the funeral. We had heard of the hearse, drawn by four horses and we fearfully looked often towards the main road. The village was some distance down towards the railway line.

Then we saw it coming, a ghostly black hearse with tassels on the sides, and magnificent horses looking so elegant in their fine polished harness. We rushed into the room. Then I stood as if rooted to the ground. Kneeling at the bedside were three women in black rocking themselves back and forth and raising their voices to the highest pitch possible, and lowering the cry like that of a wounded animal. There were no words. Some of the small children were terrified and for the second time we were brought out of the room. The hearse had arrived by this and the caoining continued until the coffin was put into the back of the hearse. That is the only time I ever witnessed this kind of mourning for the dead. Long ago it was the custom to have "hired criers" at funerals. Many Irish priests were totally against this custom and regarded wakes as places of a night's fun, of eating, drinking, playing music and smoking and continued to decry wakes until they succeeded in stopping them.

Éibhlín Dhubh Ní Chonaill

This lamenting has been carried out in almost every part of Ireland but particularly in Connacht and Munster. One such has come down in Gaelic Literature, and is called "Caoineadh Airt Úi Laoghaire". Art was murdered during the height of the Penal Days when an Irishman was not allowed to own a horse worth more than five pounds. He returned to Magh Chromtha (Macroom) after the end of the Seven Year's War, having spent some time in the Hussars in Austria under the Empress Marie Theresa. He was married to Éibhlín Dhubh Ní Chonail and they had two children and Éibhlín was pregnant with her third.

At the races in Macroom Art's horse beat the horse of Morris. Morris a Protestant, offered Art five pounds for the horse and was refused. Art was sought by Morris and so could not sleep at home. Morris gathered a group of Redcoats and they intercepted Art at Carraig an Ime at the river Lee, and shot him, 1771. The horse made his way to their home where Éibhlín was in bed. It was not long before she was kneeling at his side. The next day his body was laid out in their home and he was lamented continuously by his relations. Morris would not allow his body to be buried in consecrated ground. His body was buried outside the graveyard of Cill na Martra. Six months later his body was transferred to Mainistir Cill Chré, where the O'Laoghaire family was buried. The first caoineadh Éibhlín did is of her personal memories of Art, how she met him, what he looked like, the wonderful comfortable relationship they had and what happened the evening of his death. This lament went so hard on her that she was very near to madness.

> Mo Ghrá go daingean tú!
> Lá dá bhfaca thú
> Ag ceann tí an mhargaidh,
> Thug mo shúil aire dhuit,
> Thug mo chroí taitneamh duit,
> D'éalaíos óm charad leat
> I bhfad ó bhaile leat.

From verse ten to sixteen Art's sister in her caoining is very bitter against Éibhlín. To all appearances she is very jealous of the young widow. Then Art's father continues from there. He asks Art to rise up and go to Macroom and do all the things he did when he was alive.

This lament runs to three hundred and ninety lines[2] and it was put to music by an itinerant minstrel.

Cruiteoga : Women as patrons

Even though women held no rank in the order of the Bards they were responsible for the development of music and poetry. When singing they accompanied themselves on the harp. These women were called Cruiteoga and it has been said they studied under the Druids.[3]

There have been women patrons of literature and art. The Annals of Loch Cé record that: "Margaret, daughter of Conor O'Brien, wife of O'Rourke who died in 1513, was religious and hospitable, and helped scholars, and ollamhs, and the weak and the wretched and when she died she was buried in the monastery she had built herself to the honour of God and St. Francis, namely the Monastery of Creevlea." Another Patron of whom we will hear more, was Mrs.MacDermot Roe, who lived with her family at Alderford in North Roscommon and was the first patron of Turlough Carolan, the harper and the last of the Irish Bards.[4]

Mrs Lindon and her daughter Molly

The social revolution of the 17th century happened quietly when the folk poetry began to be preserved in manuscripts. Bardic poets were no longer in demand. An interesting item is that the mother of an early 18th century south Ulster poet, Pádraic Mac a Liondain taught her son the art of poetry making. In the mid-eighteenth century we find Padraic's own daughter Molly Lindon composing poetry in Irish. A competition between Molly and the famous poet Peadar Ó' Dóirnín reveals the early eighteenth century attitude towards women.[5] Molly was playing the harp one evening and singing songs, when O'Dóirnín entered. They held a competition to see who could compose the best verses. There was no result but as usual it was accepted that the girl was inferior. It was well known she was a better poet than her brother Padraig Óg. There must have been more women poets but they are not recorded.

Lady Morgan (Sydney Owenson) (1785-1859).

Sydney Owenson was born on Christmas day in 1785 in Dublin. Her godmother, Mary Anne Hardiman was a cousin of the historian James Hardiman. Her father (originally Mac Owen) changed his name to Robert Owenson, as he considered this anglicisation would benefit his career as an actor. Sydney said in her Memoirs (vol.1) that she was the granddaughter of Sir Malby Crofton. There is nothing to prove this.

Sidney Owenson

She tells us that her mother was an English Protestant from Shrewsbury, who had a negative assessment of Ireland 'as the land of potatoes and papists'. Her father claimed kinship to ancient Irish families. Sydney chose to follow suit. Her Irish grandmother was known in Tirawley, Co. Mayo as *Clairseach a'Bhaile*, or, The Village Harp, for the superior qualities of her musical abilities.

In the early 1800s Sydney visited Longford House, where she was a governess to young Malby Crofton. Previous to this she had been governess in Featherstone House in Dominic Street, Dublin. Here she found letters of Swift and Alexander Pope. She made use of these in her first novel - *St. Clair*. She made a great impression on the local residents of Longford House which was situated a few miles west of Ballisadare, south west of Sligo town. Sydney wrote her book *The Wild Irish Girl* while she stayed with the Croftons.

As well as being a writer Lady Morgan played the Irish Harp. John Egan of Dublin made this in 1805. She published a small collection of *Twelve Irish Melodies* in 1809. Having been a sincere admirer of O'Carolan she got a splendid bas-relief made by Hogan the sculptor and had it placed in the northern aisle of St. Patrick's Cathedral in Dublin.

In 1809, Thomas Charles Morgan M.D. lost his wife and was left with a daughter known as 'Nannie'. Sydney eventually married him. Their marriage proved a wonderful success and was a remarkably happy one. They found a house in Kildare Street, no. 25. Lady Morgan restored the house and added to it.

When Lord Morgan became ill Sydney decided he should spend his last years in his own country. They left for London in 1837. Their house was the resort of all those who were best worth knowing in London society

The following air is really *Éamon an Chnoic*, a very old traditional air. Lady Morgan took twelve of these and arranged them for piano and harp. She did not compose them. Her love of traditional airs was outstanding. This I took from Fleischmann's *Sources of Irish Music* published in 1998.

Sir Tho. Charles Morgan

SIDNEY OWENSON – *TWELVE ORIGINAL HIBERNIAN MELODIES* with English Words imitated and translated from the Works *of the Ancient Irish Bards, with an introductory Preface and Dedication by Miss S. Owenson. Arranged for the Voice with an Accompaniment for the Piano Forte.* London, 1805

4373   AH, WHO IS THAT or EMUNH A' CNUIC or NED OF THE HILLS   2

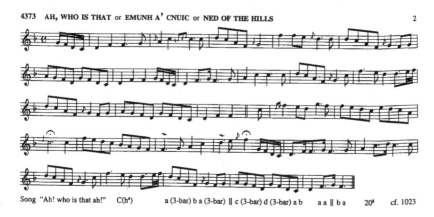

Song "Ah! who is that ah!"   C(h⁴)   a (3-bar) b a (3-bar) ‖ c (3-bar) d (3-bar) a b   a a ‖ b a   20ˢ   cf. 1023

Sydney Owenson died in 1859 surrounded by those she loved most and is buried in Brompton Cemetery.[6]

Women in the Irish Folk Song Society 1904

Charlotte Milligan Fox (1865-1916). was the principal founder of the Irish Folk Song Society in 1904. Her sister Alice Milligan was a member of its publications committee. Charlotte was born in Omagh, County Tyrone on St. Patrick's Day. Her father was a wealthy business man, Seaton F.Milligan and was a member of the Royal Irish Academy. On visits to her mother's family in Omagh she was introduced to Irish history and the Irish language and music. Her musical ability was recognised early on and she was sent to the Conservatoire in Frankfurt, the Royal College of Music in London and the Conservatoire in Milan. When she was a very little girl her father and mother took her on a trip to Sligo. To the great indignation of the long-car driver and passengers, she called out now and again " I'll shoot the Fenians". They were probably the first words she was taught to utter as her nurse was an ardent orangewoman.

Although Charlotte wrote many original songs she is remembered as one of the first song collectors of the the Irish Revival period. She was taken as a very small girl to Belfast to hear musical and operatic artists like Titiens and others. At eleven years she announced to her friends that her musical education was complete. It was probably a little girlish show off. She was always looking for more and better teaching. When she was thirteen the family went to live in Belfast. She studied in Germany for two years. She brought a songbook home from the Royal Academy of Music in London. This was Villiers Stanford's arrangement of fifty Irish airs with words by Percival Graves. It was Robert Young of Belfast, (who died at the age of ninety four) who firs

drew her attention to the works of Bunting. And so the Bunting papers were put at her disposal by Dr. Mc Rory and Lady Deane. After her death they were placed in the library of the Queens College.

Perceval Graves said Charlotte was the first to show the value of a greater specialisation in our Irish Folk Song Movement. She travelled the north and south of Ireland with pencil and music paper talking with farmers, pipers, harpers, fiddlers and ballad singers. With her phonograph she took down Irish airs and Irish words. She edited the *First Song Journal* in conjunction with Herbert Hughes. In 1911 she published the *Annals of the Irish Harpers* based on her study of the papers of Edward Bunting. In this book she gives an account of Patrick Lynch's journey into the far reaches of Co.Mayo and the hardships he endured. After this she went on a tour of the States but ill health prevented further work in this area. She returned to London where she was living with her solicitor husband and sadly she died on March 25th 1916.

Alice Milligan, sister of Charlotte Milligan Fox

Alice like her sister devoted her life to "Irish Ireland Ideals". She went to Dublin to learn Irish and met Michael Davitt, W.B. Yeats and others who would take part in the Irish Renaissance. She wrote many poems and was trying to make her living as an author. She was an enthusiastic member of the National Literary Society and the Gaelic League. She co-founded the Henry Joy McCracken Society in Belfast. She and Eithne Carbery founded and edited *The Northern Patriot*. This was a nationalist monthly journal. Alice and Eithne later founded and edited the *Sean Van Vocht* (1896-1899) This advocated social reform and separatism. They published the earliest writings of James Connolly. Influenced by Maud Gonne Alice became the organising secretary for the 1798 centenary. She helped with Sinn Féin and was associated with Inginidhe na hÉireann. She wrote the *Life of Wolfe Tone* and the *Escape of Red Hugh*. She returned to Omagh in 1932. Her famous poem:

When I was a little girl
Then the wind shaken pane sounded like drumming;
Oh ! they cried , tuck us in, the Fenians are coming!
But one little rebel there watching all with laughter,
Thought, 'when the Fenians come I'll rise and go after!'

She received an honorary D. Litt. From the National University of Ireland in 1941. She died poor and lonely in 1953 at Tycur, Omagh. The Civil War had deeply upset her and it was then she wrote her last poem on a public issue; *Till Ferdia Came.*

Éibhlín Bean Mhic Choisdealbha (1870-1962)

Éibhlín Ni Coisdealbha was a gentle soul. She wrote the preface to *Amhráin Mhuighe Seóla* in 1918 and she talks of all the people she collected songs from in Tuam and the surrounding areas and says she had no intention of offering them for publication. I am so glad she did as the all these would be lost otherwise. She consulted experts such as Rev. H.Bewerunge of Maynooth, and Dr. Charles of London. The Irish Folk Song Society offered to bring out the book. It contains traditional folk-songs from Galway and Mayo.[7]

Éibhlín was born in London in 1870. Edith Drury was her name and she was probably born in the Strand Union Workhouse in St. Pancras. Her background is not too clear except that her father was a native of Co. Limerick and her mother was Welsh. Her daughter Nuala who was well known in Tuam spoke to Ciarán Mac Mathúna on the radio some years ago and confirmed this. Éibhlín was educated through some protestant charitable society, and qualified as a teacher. Later she became principal of a Church of England school in London. She joined the Irish Literary Society, where she got to know the Yeats sisters. Éibhlín was already collecting songs from emigrants before joining the London branch of the Gaelic League when it was founded in 1896. She was the only woman on the committee. In 1902 she was one of the delegates sent to the Ard Fheis of the Gaelic League in Dublin. She went to Inis Meáin, one of the Aran Islands with Una Farrelly and they organised an aeraíocht (open air Irish festival) . She had to resign her post as principal of the school in London as she had become a Catholic.

In 1903 she came to Ireland and Sir Joseph Glynn invited her to Tuam where she got a teaching post with the Presentation nuns in Tuam. That year she married Dr. Thomas Bodkin Costello (1864-1956) who practiced medicine in Tuam during which time he studied local antiquities, history and folklore. He was a founder member of the Galway Archaeological and Historical Society. Éibhlín travelled with him while on his rounds and collected many songs. During the War of Independence she stood for Sinn Féin and was elected as District Councillor for North Galway and as a Tuam Town Commissioner. She was elected to the Senate with Alice Stopford Greene, the historian, and they both helped to establish Coláiste Connacht an all-Irish school. Both she and Jenny Wyse Power were against 'divorce' and spoke against Yeats on this question. Divorce and Matrimonial Causes Act of 1857 transferred jurisdiction from parliament to the courts. This act was never extended to Ireland, presumably because there was no demand for it. So it remained necessary for anyone seeking a divorce in Ireland to submit a private bill to parliament. The right was seldom exercised. Éibhlín had strong convictions that as women had been given the vote they must accept the responsibilities as well as the privileges. She was responsible with Jenny Wyse Power in bringing about the Senate's rejection of the Civil Servant Regulation Bill (1925) and forcing the amendment of the Juries Bill 1927, on the grounds that these bills discriminated against women. Her house was raided by the infamous Black and Tans because it was a 'safe house' for volunteers.   She acted as judge in the Sinn Féin Courts. Why are the lives of these women and many others not portrayed in our schools senior programmes letting students be aware of the great work that was done? This gentle soul as I called her in the first paragraph accomplished trojan work in her life time.

CHAPTER 4

COLLECTIONS OF RAFTERY'S SONGS BY EIBHLIN BEAN UÍ CHOISDEALBHA AND DOUGLAS HYDE

WITH THE MUSIC OF THOMAS CONNELLAN AND THE COLLECTION OF JOYCE.

This picture is of Antoine Ó Reachtabhra (1784-1835) from *Abhráin agus Dánta an Reachtabhraigh* by Douglas Hyde published in 1903 in the Irish language. Douglas Hyde was a wonderful Irish scholar and he left us a rich heritage of song and story. At the end of his preface, in that book he says "Beannacht Dé ar na sean-Ghaedhilgeoiribh! The blessings of God be upon the Irish". He was a poet, a scholar, a translator, a co-founder of the Gaelic League, a promoter of the Gaelic language and the first President of Ireland. He helped to make people aware that we all shared a common identity.

Eibhlín Ui Choisdealbha is the author of Amhráin Mhuighe Seóla, which contains eighty traditional songs from Galway and Mayo. These were published by the Irish Folk Song Society in 1918. Eibhlin and Douglas Hyde were good friends and found it a great help to compare notes on their collections. She intended that her airs would be used in the schools and Gaelic League classes in Connacht. Living in Tuam, Co. Galway she had the advantage of being in the centre of an Irish speaking district where traditional music had survived. And she acknowledged the fact that Douglas Hyde allowed her to use eight examples of his own collection of Raftery's poems.

Anthony Raftery was born in Cill Aodáin, near Coillte Mach in Co. Mayo about the year 1784. His father, who came from Céis in Co. Sligo, was a weaver by trade and reared nine children. Anthony lost his sight at nine years of age. He started to learn the fiddle and even though he never became an expert, and had a bad instrument he managed to eke out a living as he travelled from place to place in Connacht. Raftery's poems were in praise of people and places and beautiful women. He also composed political poems encouraging the people to rise against the English. He spent most of his life in Co. Galway and Clare.

One of Raftery's striking characteristcs was his hunger for knowledge. One man told Douglas Hyde that he often saw Raftery in his uncle's school sitting on the school bench listening to the teacher. One lady said he hadn't a stím of sight and that was the reason he had so much knowledge. Others said he got all from the fairies! James Hardiman from Tuam was a friend of Raftery.[1] His *Irish Minstrelsy*, was published in 1831, a book of verse in both English and in Irish. Hardiman (1782-1885) was a man of letters, a historian, author of *The History of the Town and County of Galway*. In the R.I.A. the writings of Hardiman on Raftery are the most accurate account to be had. One day Raftery heard someone ask as he had played a tune 'Who is the musician"?[2] This was his answer.

Mise Raiferti

Mise Raifteri an file,
Lán dóchais agus grádh;
Le súilibh gan solus,
Le ciúneas gan chrádh
Dul siar ar m'aistear
Le solas mo chroídhe
Fann agus tuirseach
Go deire mo slíghe,
Féach anois mé
Agus m'aghaidh ar bhalla
Ag seinnim ceol
Do phócaí follamh

Douglas Hyde had a great affection for the people, the poetry and the land of Connacht. His earliest recollections were of Kilmactranny where his father had been appointed a minister. However it was the custom of the time that the first child of the family should be born in the maternal home of the grandparents. And so his mother Maria Meade Oldfield went home to the Glebe House of Kilkeevan parish in Castlerea. Here Douglas was born in 1860. His mother returned with her new baby and so Douglas had the freedom of the glens and the fields at the most impressionable time of his life. That lovely song we all learned going to school 'San nGleann in ár Togadh Me' was composed by him about the Kilmactranny glens.

San nGleann 'nn ár Tógadh Me

O áit go háit ba bhreágh mo shiúbhal
A's b'árd mo léim air bhárr an t-sléibh';
San uisge fíor budh mhór mo dhúil,
'S budh bheó mo chroidhe I lár mo chléibh;
Mar chois an gheirrfhiadh bhí mo chos,
Mar iarann gach alt a's féith,
Bhí 'n sonas rómham, anall 's abhus,
Ann san ngleann 'nn ar tógadh mé.

Budh chuma liom-sa fear ar bith,
Budh chuma an domhan iomlán,
Mar rith an fhiadh bhí mo rith,

Mar shruth an t-sléibhe dul le fán;
A's ní raibh rud ar bith sa domhan
Nach ndearnas (dá m'budh mhaith liom é);
Do léim mo bhád air bhárr na n-abhann
Ann san ngleann 'nn ar tógadh mé.

Gach nidh d'á bh-facas le mo shúil
Bhí sé, dar liom,ar dath an óir,
Is anamh dhearcainn air mo chúl,
Ach dul air aghaidh le misneach mór;
Do leanfainn-sé gan stad gan sgith
Mo rún (dá g-cuirfinn rómham-sa é)
Do bhéarfainn, dar liom, air an ngaoith,
Ann san ngleann 'nn ar tógadh mé.

Ní h-amhlaidh tá sé liom anois!
Do bhí mé luath, 's tá mé mall;
Is é, mo léun ! an aois do bhris
Sean neart mo chroidhe a's lúth mo bhall.
Do chaill mé mórán; 's fuair mé fios
air mhórán; Óch! Ní sásughadh é!
Mo leun! Mo leun! gan mise arís óg
'san ngleann 'nn ar tógadh mé.

On a recent tour of Sligo and Roscommon, June 1999 we had the good fortune of meeting Dr. Hugh Gibbons of Keadue who brought us around that beautiful area of Ballyfarnon, Keadue, the ancient Ballindoon Dominican Priory, Kilmactranny, Arigna, the Curlew Mountains and the Lough Arrow Research Project in Highwood.[3] We traced Carolan's footsteps throughout the area and visited the home and burial place of Terence Mac Donogh (better known as The Counsellor).This particular part of the country is not developed industrially, and hopefully never will be. The trip through its lanes and boreens brought an exciting view around each bend. We visited the Glebe House where Douglas Hyde was brought up for the first eight or nine years of his life. The house is large and well cared by its present owner.

It was near his own home in Frenchpark that Hyde heard an old man singing Killeadan, or Co. Mayo as he leant across the half-door of his humble home. The song went to the heart of Hyde and he moved to the door and said "will you teach me those two verses"? The old man did but he did not know the origin of the air or who composed it. Fifteen years after that Douglas Hyde was studying the Irish language in the Royal Irish Academy.[4] To his amazement he came across the song and only then realised that Raftery was the author. In Craughwell he was told that Raftery had died in the house of Diarmuid O'Cluanáin, a small farmer and that his songs were written in a notebook but the man who had the book was gone to Newfoundland. Finally after much searching Lady Gregory found the book. It had been written in good Irish fifty years before. Lady Gregory borrowed it for Hyde and he copied seventeen poems. There were twenty-two of Raftery's poems in this book.

Hyde went back to the R.I.A. in Dublin where he found twenty-five more of Raftery's songs. He got eight more from a friend in Galway, Eoin O'Neachtan. He got a further five from Fr. Clement O'Lúghnaigh in the monastery in Loughrea who had taken down the words from an old man twenty years before.   After that he borrowed a manuscript from Fr. O'Flynn in Tuam, a friend of his who had written down many of Raftery's poems. Dr. Hyde was a happy man when he had this amount gathered. The remainder he got from various friends. The following are some of these songs which are great favourites especially in the west.[5]

The version here of Cill Aodáin was collected by Eibhlín Bean Uí Choisdealbha and verified by Dr. Hyde. It is in praise of Raftery's native home where everything grows: blackberries, raspberries and fruit of every kind. There is planting and ploughing here: oats, barley, flax, and rye. There are kilns and mills working. Trees of all kinds grow: sycamore, beech, hazel, fir, ash, box and holly, yew, birch and rowanberry. One hundred years later, the poverty of Coillte Magh and Foxford was extreme and far removed from the days of Raftery.

Cill Aodáin

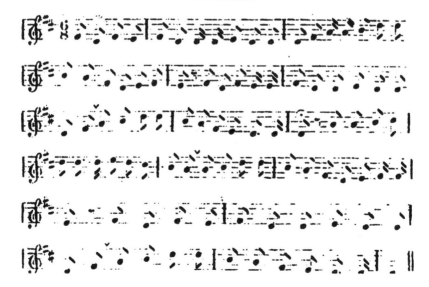

Anois teacht an earraigh, beidh an lá ag dul 'un síneadh
A's tar éis na féil Brígdhe árdóchadh mo sheól ,
Ó chuir mé i mo cheann é, ní stopfaidh mé choidhche
Go seasfaidh mé síos i lár Chondae Mhuigheo.
I gClár Cloinne Mhuiris, do bhéas mé an chéad oídhche,
'S i mBaile taobh thíos de, thosóidh mé ag ól
Go Coillte Mach rachad go ndéanfadh cúaint míosa ann,
I bhfogus dá mhíle go Béal an Áth mhóir.

Towards the Eve of St.Brigid the days will be growing
The Cock will be crowing and a home wind shall blow
And I never shall stop, but shall ever be going
Till I find myself roving through the County Mayo,
The first night in Claremorris I hope to put over,
And in Balla below it the cruiskeens shall flow;
In Coillte Mach then I'll be living in clover
Near the place that my home is and the house that I know.

Fágaim le h-udhachta go n-éirigheann mo chroidhe-se
Mar éirigheanns an ghaoth, nó mar sgapas an ceó
Nuair smuainighim ar Chearra a's ar Ghaillin taobh thíos de
Ar Sgeachtach a'Mhíle no ar Phláinéad Mhuigh Eo.
Cill Aodáin an baile a bhfásann gach nidh ann,
Tá sméara 's súbh-chraobh ann a's meas ar gach sórt,
'S dá mbéinn-se mo sheasamh I gceart-lár mo dhaoine
D'imtheóchadh an aois díom agus bhéinn arís óg.

I solemnly aver it, that my heart rises up
Even as the wind rises or as the mist disperses
When I think about Carra and about Gallen down from it,
Upon the Mile-bush or upon the plains of Mayo.
Killeadan (is) the village in which everything grows,
There are blackberries and raspberries in it and fruit of every kind,
And if I were only to be standing in the middle of my people
The age would go from me and I should be young again.

Tá gach uile shórt adhmaid dá'r chóir do chur síos ann,
Bíonn sciamór 's beech ann, coll, giubhais, a's fuinnseóg,
Box agus cuileann, iúbhar, beith, agus caorthan
'S an ghlas-dair d'a ndéantar bád long a's crann –seoil.

An Logwood, Mahogony, 's gach adhmad d'á daoirse,
'S an fíor mhaide dhéanfadh gach uile ghleus ceóil
Oltóir(?) 's sgeach gheal ann d'á gearradh 's d'a snoíghmeadh
'S an tslat ann do dhéanfadh cis cléibh agus lóid.

There is every sort of timber that it were fit to put down there,
There is sycamore and beech in it, hazel, fir and ash,
Box and holly, yew, birch and rowan berry
And the green oak which has made boat and ship and mast;
The log-wood,mahogony and every timber no matter how expensive
And the fior-mhaide which would make every musical instrument ;
Óltoir and white hawthorn a cutting and a hewing
And the rod there that would make basket creels and lods.

Fághann dílleachta 's baintreabhach cabhair a's réidhteach
Slighe bidh, a's éadhaigh, a's talamh gan cíos,
Sgoláiridhe bochta sgriobh sgoil,agus leigheann ann,
Lucht iarrtha na déirce ann, ag tarraing 's ag triall.
Sháraigh sé an domhan ina h-uile dheagh-thréithribh
Thug Raifterí an chraobh dó ar a bfacaidh sé riamh,
Sé deireadh na cainte: Saol fad ag Franc Taffe ann
Sliocht Loinnsigh na féile nár choigil an fhiadhach.

The orphan and the widow get assistance and redemption,
A way to get food and clothes and land without rent;
Poor scholars get writing and schooling and learning there,
And the people who ask alms are drawing and journeying thither
It overcame the world for all its good qualities
And Raftery has awarded it the branch over all that he ever saw.
The end of the talk is this: Long life to Frank Taffe in it
The descendant of the Lynch of hospitality who never spared the hunt.

The Frank Taffe referred to in the last verse was a wealthy man who lived in the local "Big House".   He was of the branch of Sir William Taffe of Ballymote who got lands in 1592 during the time of Queen Elizabeth.[6] William's son Sir John Taffe was made Baron of Ballymote in 1603. Frank employed Raftery's father as a weaver and he became Raftery's patron when the latter lost his sight. On Taffe's land there was a large boghole which Raftery, though blind, could cross. He had counted the number of steps from a certain point to a flagstone at the edge of the hole. After running the required number of steps he could make the leap successfully.

But he brought the anger of Taffe upon himself, when one night there was feasting and drinking in Taffe's "Big House." As the drink got scarce Taffe sent a servant to the town on horseback for more supplies. The servant asked Raftery to go with him. Raftery took Taffe's best horse and the servant knew that if both horses kept together all would be well. Somehow or other they got separated and Raftery going at top speed, came to a sharp turn on the road. The horse could not stop in time and he went in a jump across into the bog hole and was drowned. Raftery came safe but Padraig Ó'hAoidh one of Hyde's informants said this was the reason Raftery left Cill Aodáin. Taffe put him out and he wandered the roads of Galway from that out as a travelling minstrel. It has been said he was an advocate for the United Irishmen at the time so when he reached Tuam he was not approved of. Siobhan was his wife's name but Peatsaí Ó Callanáin another of Hyde's informants said they were not married at all. They had two children a son and a daughter. The son played the fiddle and was said to have joined a circus. Siobhan and Raftery separated. The daughter was known years later as a small old lady going from place to place with a little knapsack selling pins and needles and thread. Some people said that Raftery composed Cill Aodáin in order to make peace with Taffe but that Taffe was annoyed because Raftery waited until the last verse before he mentioned his name. So it appears Raftery could not please everyone!

Raftery's religious poems are to be found in the Royal Irish Academy. In the National Library Manuscripts Room in Dublin there are notes about Raftery from the nineteenth century by Séan Mag Fhloinn.There are also twenty-two poems of Raftery's written phonetically by Pádraig Ó Comain. The originals are in the possession of Mrs Delia Commins of Turlough Mór Co. Galway.

Another of Raftery's songs collected both by Douglas Hyde and Eibhlín Uí Coisdealbha was Bridín Bhéasaigh.

Bridín Bhéasaigh

Phósfainn brídín bhéasaigh, gan cóta uirrthí ná léine
A stór mo chroí dá mbféidir liom, do throisgfinn duit naoi dtráth
Gan bia gan deoch gan aon chuid, ar oileán i Loch Éirne
Dfhonn mé is tú bheith in éinfeacht go réighfimis ár gcás.
A ghrúaigh ar dath na gcaor chon, a chúaichín bháirr an t-sléibhe,
Do ghealladh ná déan bheugach ach éirigh roimh an lá
'S in aimhdheoin dlighe na cléire go dtógfainn tú mar chéile
'S a Dhia, nar dheas an scéal sin, duine ag éaló lena ghrá.

Do gheit mo chroidhe le buaidhreamh, agus sgannraidh mé naoí n-uaire
Ar mhaidin úd do chualaidh mé nach raibh tú rómham le fághail,

'S a liacht lá faoi shuairceas chaith mise 's tú in uaigneas
'S gan neach ar bith d'ár gcúmhdach, ach an crúisgín 's é ar an gclár.
Dá bhfághainn amach do thuairaisc, dá dtéightfeá go bonn cruaiche,
Rachadh an sgéal ró chruaidh orm ,nó leanfainn do mo ghrá
'S go mbfhearr (liom) sínte suas leat 's gan fúinn ach fraoch a's luachair,
Ná bheith 'g éisteacht leis na cuacaibh, bhíos ag siubhal ag éirighe lá.

Though shoeless, shirtless, grieving, foodless too my Bridin,
Surely I'll not leave you nine meals I'd fast for you
Upon Lough Erne's islands, no food no drink beside me
Still hoping I may find you, my children to be true.
O Cheek so blush- abounding, O Berry of the mountain,
Your promise, love is sounding forever in my ear.
In spite of cleric's frowning I'd take you as I found you;

It's I who would go bounding, eloping with my dear.
I frightened in my heart, for it leapt nine times and started,
That morning that you parted and were not to be found,
And all the happy evening I spent beside my dearest,
And no one came between us and the jug was on the ground.
I'll travel through the island still seeking for your tidings
And hard it will betide me, if I find not my love.
I'd sooner sit beside you on rushes through the night time,
Than listen to the finest of the birds in the grove.

There are various versions, but this one I picked out from the tape on Radio na Gaeltachta made by Máire Ní Chéidigh, from Connemara in 1986.[7] Dr. Hyde got the story of the poem from Fr. Clement O' Lúghnaigh in the monastery in Loughrea in Co. Galway. Bridín and her father and mother came from Castlebar to Loughrea. Bridín got employment as a servant girl in the house of the local Minister, Medlicott. Raftery visited this house often and he and Bridín became great friends. After he had been away for awhile, he returned to find Bridín had moved as housekeeper to Killaloo with the Minister. His grief was deep. He went into a little hut on the edge of Loughrea and he poured his heart out for the girl he said he loved.

Peigín Mistéal

Mrs. Costello of Tuam Co. Galway got this song from Bridget Forde of Tuam who said she learned it from her father.[8] She gives the complete version of the words.

'B'ait liom bean d'imreóchadh cleas , 's nach gclisfeadh ar a grádh,
Shiúbhalfadh asteach le greann ar fhear,Is nach seasfadh leis san tsráid,
Béilín deas 's milse blas ná mil na mbeachf faoi Cháisg,
Cúl trom, tais, fionn, fáinneach glas, 's í Peigidh tá mé 'rádh.

A Stór mo chroí ná tréig do mhian ach breathnuigh 'steach sán gcás,
Nuair thiucfas an tslíghe béidh ól ar fhíon 's ní baol dúinn choiche bás.
A bhláth na gcraobh nach cruaidh an scéal munab tú tá dham i ndán
Ar uaisle an tsaol dá mbéinn mo rí is leat do chraithfinn lámh.'

'I like a maid who's not afraid, but loves so well a man,
She goes with him, both out and in, and loves him all she can.
A mouth fine, small, and sweet withal as honey in the spring,
And heavy hair flung backwards there, 'tis Peggy fair I sing.

Treasure of my heart, do not forsake thy desire,
but look into the case, when the means shall come,
there shall be drinking and wine, and no danger of death to us for ever.
Oh blossom of the branches is it not a hard story
if it be not you are laid out by fate for me, over the nobility of the world,
If I were king, it is with you I would shake hand.

Máire Ní Eidhin nó An Pabhsae Glégeal

Raftery spoke of this beautiful lady who lived more than one hundred years before his time in the west of Ireland. She lived beside Gort Inse Guaire and the ruins of the house at Baile Uí Liagh could be seen in Raftery's time. It was in the barony of Kiltartan. An old lady said to Lady Gregory "I have never seen or will I ever see anyone so beautiful as Máire." Twelve men proposed to Máire in one day. She did not marry any of them. Many loved her but she died young and in poverty. She had hair of a golden colour and was always dressed in her Sunday best. Raftery praises Máire the most beautiful girl that ever lived. A nobleman was in love with her but he deserted her and she died a very young girl. Douglas Hyde got the words from Tomás Uí Eidhin a relative of Máire. He was a fine traditional singer. Petrie also collected this air. It is no. 1542 in his collection.

The Mass-path led to the Lord of Graces,
The skies were rainy and the wind was high,
Beside Kiltartan I met a maiden

Whose eyes waylaid me with sudden wile.
I gave her greetings polite and stately,
She answered gracious as any queen,
'O Raftery' she said 'could fate be kinder?
Now step beside me to Ballylee.

'Dul chuig an Aifreann dam le toil na nGrásta,
Do bhí an lá 'a báistighe, agus d' árduigh gaoth,
Casadh an ainnir liom le taobh Chilltartain
Agus thuit me láithreach I ngrá le mnaoi.
Labhair me léi go múinte mánla
'S do réir   cáileacht 's eadh d'fhreagair si
'Seurd dúirt sí,'Raifteiri tá m'inntin sásta
'gus gluais sí go lá liom go Baile Liagh.

Tá a folt ag casadh léi ar dhath na sméara
'Na soillse rae-gheal 'na diaidh san drúcht,
An solus lasta ina brollach glégeal,
A d'fhág na céadtha fear i ngalar dúbhach.
A brághaid is gile 'ná sneachta séidte
Is lúthmhar éadtrom a cosa ag siúbhal
A's mo rígh dá mbéinn-se mar Iuilius Caesar
Do dhéanfainn réidhteach le bláth na n-ubhall.

Anach Chuain

A tragic accident happened on Lough Corrib in Co. Galway in the year 1828. Thirty-one people and ten sheep with other goods were going to the fair in Galway and went on board a very old boat at Annaghdown. The boat was rotten and within two miles from Galway a leak was sprung. One of the men plugged it with his coat and pressing with his heel he drove the whole plank out of the boat. In a few seconds nineteen of them were drowned, eleven men and eight women. They were only a short distance from land. Twelve were rescued by another boat.

This terrible event brought weeping and sadness and horror to the people of Connacht. Raftery said that to his dying day he would never forget this tragic happening and he composed most of the verses. Dr. Hyde got some of the verses from Próinsias Ó Conchubhair who heard them from an old lady who lived in Annaghdown. He got the remainder from a blind old man from Tuam.

If my health is spared I'll be long relating
Of that boat that sailed out of Annaghdown
And the keening after the mother and father
And child by the harbour, the mournful croon;
O King of Graces who died to save us,
'Twere a small affair for but one or two
But a boat load bravely in calm day sailing
Without storm or rain to be swept to doom.

'Má fhaghaim-se sláinte is fada bhéidheas trachtadh
Ar an méid do báitheadh as Anach Cuan
'S mo thruagh amárach gach athair is máthair
Bean a's páiste tá a' sileadh súl.
A Rí na ngrásta cheap neamh a's Párrthas
Nár beag an tabhacht dúinn beirt ná triúr
Ach, lá chomh breá leis, gan gaoith ná báisteach,
Lán a' bháid aca a scuabadh ar siúbhal!

The song was sometimes known as Cnoch a Déaláin the name of the place at which the fair was held.

Douglas Hyde was about fifteen years old when he began to jot down in a note-book odd scraps about people around the Ballaghaderreen-Frenchpark area. This was the beginning of his distinguished career as a folklorist. In his preface to the Religious songs of Connacht he says he found poems, prayers, 'paidirs', petitions, 'orthas' charms, stories, blessings and curses, all of which he published. He never came across a single song which cursed people of the Protestant religion something which surprised him considering the harshness of the Penal Laws. But the country people often cursed the 'Galls' (the people in the province of Connacht who spoke English).

Connacht gave to Ireland probably her best religious poet – Donogh O'Daly who was Abbot of Boyle. He died in 1244. The following poem by O'Daly was noted by Hyde from a 'travelling man' near Belmullet in the west of Mayo county.

Ná tréig mo Theagasg

Ná tréig mo theagasg a Mhic
Cidh baogh'lach lá an chirt do chách
Ag scaoileadh dhóibh o'n tsliabh
Rachfaidh tú le Dia na ngrás.

Do not forsake my teaching my son
Though dangerous the day of right to all,
On their being let loose down the mountain
Thou shalt go with God of the graces.

Seachain leisge, craos 's drúis,
Do chroidh a's do shúil ag saint,
Seachain díomas, fearg 's fuath
'S béidir ar neamh shuas ar neamh gan chaill.

Shun sloth, shun greed, shun sensual fires,
(Eager desires of men enslaved).
Anger and pride and hatred shun,
Till heaven be won, till man be saved.

The following curse was collected by Hyde in Co. Galway. It's the curse of a poor blind man who came to the door of a big house and asked for a drink. The woman of the house was an English woman and she asked the servant what he wanted. Then she said "Water is good enough for a blind beggar". The blind man understood what she said and gave this reply.

Mallacht an Daill

Im ná raibh ar do bhainne,
Clumh ná raibh ar do lachain,
Siubhal ná raibh ar do leanbh,
Agus feannadh ar do bhó.

A Blind Man's curse.
Your milk may no butter crown,
On your ducks may there come no down,
May your child never walk the ground,
Be your cows where the flayer flays.

Úna Bhán

This is a beautiful song composed by Tomás Láidir Mac Coisdealbha (Costello) about the time of the restoration in 1660. He lived near the remains of the Costello Castle at Tullaghan Rock, on the Sligo side of Ballaghaderreen about two miles out. Tomás was, according to tradition, a brother of Dudley the Rapparee who was killed on Bárr na Laidhre (or Bárr na Cúige where Connacht Airport now stands.) Tomás Láidir fought bravely against the Cromwellian forces and performed great feats of strength in a fierce battle at the Curlew Mountains, during which he saved the life of Turlough Mac Dermot's son and heir. When Tómas died he was buried in the same graveyard as Úna. And tradition has it that there grew an ash tree out of Una's grave and another out of the grave of Tomás Laidir and they inclined towards one another until the two tops met. Dr. Hyde wrote in 1933 that Jasper Tully, editor of the Roscommon Herald, told him that in 1865 he saw the trees entwined over their graves.

Úna Bhán.

A Úna bhán bhán is granna an luidhe ort
ar leabhaidh caol árd ameasg na mílte corp
Muna dtagaidh tú fáidh orm a stáid-bhean a bhí riamh gan locht
Ní thíucfaidh mé chun na háite seo go bráth ach aréir is anocht"

O fair haired Úna, ugly is the lying that is upon you,
On a bed narrow and high among the thousand corpses
If you do not come and give me a token, Ó stately woman, who was ever without a fault
I shall not come to this place forever, but last night and to night.

A Úna, a rúin, is tú a mhearaigh mo chiall
Úna, a rúin, is tú a chuaidh idir mé is Dia
A Úna, a rúin, a lúib chumhra chasta na gciabh,
B'hfearr dhomsa bheith gan súile ná t'fhaicsint ariamh.

O fair Úna, it is you who have set astray my senses;
O Úna, it was you who went close between me and God,
O Úna fragrant branch, twisted little curls of ringlets,
Was it not better for me to be without eyes than ever to have seen you.

The Costelloes had three strongholds; one at Kilcolman, of which a trace is not now to be had, one at Tullaghan Rock, the ruins of which is covered in briars and shrubs and the Castlemore Castle of which very little is left. Robert Costello built a new house, shown above, in 1867.

An Droighneáin Donn

Eibhlín Uí Choisdealbha of Tuam got this song from Maggie Hession. It is to be found in James Hardiman's (a Tuam man) "Irish Minstrelsy," in O'Daly's "Poets and Poetry of Munster" p.238, in Hyde's "Love Songs of Connacht, in Petrie's collection No.451 and in O'Neills No. 31, 32 and 33.

Síleann céad fear gur leo féin mé nuair olaim lionn,
'S theidhean dá dtrian síos díom nuair smaoinighim air do chomhrádh liom
Do chum is míne 'ná an síoda air Shliabh Uí Fhloinn
's go bhfuil mo ghrádh-sa mar bhláth an áirne air an droighneáin donn.

A hundred men think I am theirs when I drink beer,
And two thirds of them go down from me
When I remember your conversation with me;
Your form smoother than the silk that is on the mountains of O'Flynn,
And sure my love is like the blossom of the sloe on the brown blackthorn.

Moll Dubh an Ghleanna

Dr. Hyde tells us he got this song from an old man from near Ballaghaderreen called Walter Sherlock. He says there is a great difference between it and the one in James Hardiman's book. Hyde and Mrs Costello compared notes on this air. He says that Shawn Ó' Dálaigh – a man who never received sufficient praise for his Munster songs, said that it was "Ned Ryan of the hills", or "Éamon an Chnoic" who composed this song between 1730 and 1740. Hyde goes on to say that he got another version of this song called Pol Dubh a' Ghleanna from Donal Considine, a Clare man.

It is with Dark Moll of the valley, my heart is laid up in keeping
It is she got neither blame nor shame, it is courteously, mannerly, beautifully,
She said to me in the morning, go and see me not forever,
There is no handsome youth from Munster to Tuam and Galway
Or from that to Leyney of the O'Hara
Attending upon the most beautiful Dark Woman.

Is ag Bean Dubh an ghleanna tá mo ghrá i dtaisce,
Is I nach bhfuair guth ná náire,is caoidheamhail múintearais
Dúirtsí liom ar maidin, imigh is ná feuch go bráth mé
Níl óganách deas o Múmhain go Tuaim 's go Gaillimh,
Ná ó sin go Laighnibh úi hÉaghra, nach bhfuil triall chum an ghleanna
Ar eachraibh slíocaibh sleamhain, (Ag) feitheamh ar an mBean dubh is áille.

Pol Dubh an Ghleanna

Tá bó agam ar shliabh,is fada mé 'nna dhiaidh
a's do chaill mé mo chiall le nódhchar,
D'á seóladh soir (a's)siar, a's gach áit a ngabhann an ghrian,
no go bh'filleann sí aniar ('san) tráthnóna.
Nuair féachaim se anúnn 'san mbaile
a bhfuil mo rún tuiteann ó mo shuil ghlais deora
A Dhia mhóir na ngrás tabhair fuasgailt ar mo chás
a's gur Bean Dubh a d'fhág fá bhrón mé.

Upon the mountain brow I herd a lowing cow,
(and my sense is gone now through a maiden);
I drive her east and west, and where're the sun shines best,
to return with her white milk laden
But when I look above, to the village of my love,
My grey eyes fill in their dreaming;
O Mighty God of grace, take pity in my case,
'Tis the Dark Girl left them streaming.

Mardhna Luimnich

Neales' collection of the most Celebrated Irish Tunes was first published in 1726. Marbhna Luimnigh first appeared in this book. This lonesome march reminds us of the sorrow of the Irish when their hopes were dashed after the first Battle of Limerick. It was composed by Thomas Connellan of Cloonamahon, Co. Sligo. Thomas, Myles O'Reilly and William Connellan (also of Cloonamahon) were well-known harpers of the late seventeenth century. Thomas spent twenty years in Scotland and returned home in 1689. He visited a friend - a Mr Bailey, agent to the Earl of Bath at Bourchiers's Castle near Lough Gur Co. Limerick. He died there and was buried in Teampall Nua. This graveyard is called Reilig na bhFilí, - the cemetery of the poets. In 1991 the Lough Gur & District Historical Society put up a plaque in his memory. According to tradition Thomas had composed seven hundred airs which he played on the harp. Very few of them are preserved.

Francis O'Neill tells us that a banshee wailed from the top of Carraig na g-Colur while his funeral procession was passing to the burial ground. The mournful cry of the wild pigeons, from which the rock takes its name, may account for this fancy.

Ode to O'Connellan, the Irish Harper

Spirit of Mindrelsy!
Supreme o'er Erin's bards thy sway.
To thee the silvery sounds belong,
The thrilling sympathies of song,
The warblings of an angel's sphere
That Europe's minstrels when they hear,
Overpowered –enchanted –pine away –
And yield the palm to thee

In vain do mighty kings
Invite the world to bardic feats;
To try the mastery of thy art.
To fire the soul or melt the heart;
Immortal one! thy glowing hand
The wilder music of the land
Hath silenced. – Echo but repeats
The magic of thy strings.

Sighle Bheag Ní Chonnallain

P.W.Joyce from whose book called Ancient Irish Music the above tune came spent most of his life in the Ballyhoura Hills where he was nurtured in an atmosphere of tradition, music and singing. He wrote down as many airs as he could get. Then he came to Dublin to live and got a copy of the prospectus of the Society for the Preservation and

Publication of the Melodies of Ireland. He was very interested and called upon Petrie the president of that organisation. They became good friends. Joyce gave many of his airs to Petrie who always acknowledged his indebtedness to Joyce but on Petrie 's death in 1866 Joyce decided to publish his own collection. Then in 1873 by which time he was President of the society he published Ancient Irish Music and Songs containing 842 Irish airs and songs unpublished before this. This interesting work is made up of 3 separate collections – 492 airs from himself. The second was the Ford MSS., compiled by William Forde a distinguished Cork musician and had 256 items and the third with 157 tunes comprised John Edward Pigott 's collection. Pigott was a native of Dublin. Both he and Forde had died before they could publish their work.

William Forde took a setting of three tunes - Sighle Bheag Ní Chonnallain, The Owenmore and Kesh Corran which he collected from Hugh O'Beirne, a skilled fiddler from Ballinamore, Co.Leitrim. Forde had spent quite long periods in Sligo, Galway Mayo and Leitrim. The Owenmore setting by Forde is one of Connellan's. The words can be found in the Co. Sligo reference library.

Cloonamahon, where Forde probably trod in the footsteps of Connellan is a place full of soul, and draíocht. When standing at Cloonamahon House you are on a level with the spire of the church in Collooney with a magnificent view of the countryside. The Owenmore river meanders in and out of Templehouse lands, Annaghmore and around to Cloonamonagh to the Wyndy turn where it turns the bend and flows towards Collooney (see The Wyndy Turn C.D. by Dan Healy joined by Ciarán O'Raghallaigh). In bad weather the river rises and the U- turn can be seen clearly, as the river joined by the Uinsin and the Owenbeg flows into Ballisadare Bay.

The Owenmore

From out the lake at Templehouse
A babbling Brook emerges-
A sturdy babe and masculine,
He gambols by the verges
Of farms and lawns and churchyard walls
He tumbles over ledges,
Acquiring strength with every bound,
He sways the verdant sedges.
Soon childhood's pranks are laid aside
And lusty youth discloses
Fresh feats of strength, as "Owenmore"
Each obstacle deposes.
With dauntless mien, he durst invade
The stronghold of O'Hara---
Styled "Lord of Leyney" , and akin
To bygone chiefs of Tara.
Then gliding 'round Ardcotton Glebe—
The Church full well respecting—
He moderates his headless gait,
Demurely genuflecting.
Once safely past the Parson's door
He vows he's no man's vassal.
And hastens down 'longside the town,
Towards Mac Donagh's Castle.
Beside the Hollow Mill.
And plunges headlong underneath
The bridge below the hill.
For now supreme all-conquering love
Accelerates his stride,
As joyously he presses on
To clasp his winsome bride.

Long ago there were many mills along the rivers. There were three mills on the Owenmore at Collooney, mills at Ardcree, and the flourmills at Ballisadare owned by Yeats's grandparents the Pollexfens. The life of the villages revolved around the mills. The Owenmore passed Riverstown, Coopers Hill, went around Markree Castle and entered the ocean near St. Feicin's Church. The draíocht of this river journey brings calmness to an already beautiful area.

The barony of Corran takes it's name from Coran, a harper of the Tuatha De Danaan, who was granted the territory in recognition of his merit. In the parish of Toomour, the most interesting point is the Hill of Keash. It is 1,163 feet above sea level. We hear of it in Ossianic literature. It is said that Diarmuid and Gráinne lived there before Diarmuid was killed while hunting the wild boar of Benbulben.

An important battle was fought at Keash in 971, between the Northmen and the Connachtmen. The latter were defeated. About sixty feet from the old church are ruins, said to be of the original church. It is called the Altar. Here those who fell at the battle of Keash are said to be buried. It is one of the beauty spots of the county. Small wonder with such a history that music is part of the inheritance of Keash. We have it in folklore that the fairy music coming from the openings on the hills of Keash often enchanted the listener on a sunny day.

Carolan the Harper *Courtesy of the National Gallery of Ireland*

CHAPTER 5

CAROLAN I - LIFE

Turlough Carolan was born in 1670 and lived until 1738.[1] He was the son of John Carolan a descendant of an ancient tribe of East Breifni, a district now forming part of the counties of Meath and Westmeath. John, grandson of Shane Grana O'Carolan "chief of his Sept "in 1607, was dispossessed during the wars of James 1 and reduced to a state of poverty. Patrick Carolan, the bard's uncle had in 1691, 300 acres in Nobber parish and his cousin Neale Carolan had 325 acres in Stackallen parish. The bard's father and family being homeless emigrated from their native spot and went to Ballyfarnon in Co.Roscommon where the MacDermot Roe family were landowners at that time. Arigna was part of their estate. Here Carolan's father got employment in the iron works owned by the MacDermotroes. Mrs MacDermotroe, who was one of the Fitzgeralds of Turlough, Co. Mayo, realised that young Carolan had a gift for music so she got a harper in the area to teach him.

At the age of eighteen he got smallpox and was totally deprived of his sight.Then he decided to earn his living by music, and at the age of twenty-two he began by visiting the houses of the surrounding gentry. He had already made friends with Denis O'Conor who was descended from Turlough Mór O'Conor, King in Ireland and who was living at Knockmore near Ballyfarnon having lost his inheritance at Belanagare in Co. Roscommon.The friendship with Carolan lasted all their lives.

Gaelic civilisation up to this time, was, from a cultural point of view, in the hands of the court poets who were the product of the Bardic schools. The function of the poet and harper was clear. The poetry was written down and preserved by the noble houses in books of poetry called Dunairí. All had changed however before Carolan's time. He has been called 'The Last of the Irish Bards.' He visited and composed tunes for the Gaelic Chieftains as well as for the supplanters. He made no distinction between them.

The social conditions in Ireland in the time of Carolan, especially in Connacht, left much to be desired. The landlords lived in the 'Big House'. Protestants owned some of these. As far as the gentry were concerned, be they Catholic or Protestant the harp was the principal instrument and it was much in demand at weddings and funerals. The horse was the most reliable mode of travel. Roads were mere tracks. Many of the landlords did not have a great relationship with their tenants.

Carolan was as poor as any of the Irish and it was his gift of music, which enabled him to survive. His friends were numerous and many of his patrons became his friends.[2] The harp or cruit undoubtedly enjoyed pride of place in ancient Ireland something whioh continued into the eighteenth century. It is coming into its own again in these modern times.

Following in Carolan's footsteps in the summer of 1999 we drove from Castlebaldwin across the historical route by Lough Arrow. The sun was shining, the people were friendly and informative and our expectations were high. We drove to the end of Ballyfarnon and direct to Alderford House.

There was no one home. This two-storey house is very neglected and we were sad for the memory of those wonderful people who have gone. Many of the magnificent trees were blown down in the recent storm, in spring 1999. The bedroom in which Carolan died is above the high pillars of the great front door. It was a relief to come back to the beautiful village of Ballyfarnon and talk to a group of happy school children that knew all about Carolan. We took photos of them at the foot of the Josie MacDermott memorial. We then went to see Carolan's grave at Kilronan. He is buried in the MacDermot Roe vault. Thousands visit his grave every year and the Carolan festival is held at Keadue at the end of every summer.

Alderford House

After many years travelling from place to place in Connacht Carolan in failing health decided to return to Alderford. Having said farewell to the Maguires he went to Counsellor Brady and stayed there a few nights. He was actually at Tempo when he felt himself getting weak. He returned to Alderford and met Mrs. Mac Dermotroe in the hall. He said he had come home to die. In Irish these are his words "Tháinic mé anso tar éis a ndeachas tríd, chum bás d'fhagháil is an mbaile fá dheire, mar a bhfuaras an chéad fhoghluim, agus an chéad ghearrán." His doctors Dr. John Staffard and Dr. Duigenan were there.

Sixty clergymen attended Carolan's funeral. The wake lasted four days. On Saturday 25th March 1738 Charles O'Connor wrote in one of his note books, ("Turlough O'Carolan, the wise master and chief musician of the whole of Ireland ,died today and was buried in the O'Duigenans ' Church of Kilronan ,in the 68th year of his age, May his soul find mercy ,for he was a moral and a religious man."[3]

During all this time the Penal Code which began in 1695 continued throughout Carolan's lifetime. However a few Catholic lawyers like Terence McDonogh who had been in practice before 1691 were allowed to continue to practice. So it came about that with the aid of Terence and Lord Taffe and Lord Kingston, Denis O'Conor finally recovered almost all of his lands at Belanagare in 1720.

Terence Mac Donogh, "the great counsellor", a personal friend of Carolan represented the borough of Sligo in King James's Irish Parliament in 1689. He was a most distinguished Irishman of his day, a soldier, lawyer, poet and patron of poets. He held the rank of Captain in Colonel Dillon's regiment in the Irish army of King James and commanded Ballymote Castle. He wrote the preface to Roderick O'Flahertys *Ogygia* at the time when O'Flaherty author of the first history of Connacht, was neglected by the rest of his countrymen.[4] Carolan composed a tune as well as an elegy for McDonogh.

Lament for Terrence McDonogh

"Táim dubh-chroideach go leór is níl súgaigh éin mo ghlóir,
Is níl sians in mo gháire fá do bhás, 'Thorlaigh Óig!
Árd-fhlaith na seód, a bhfuair sár-chlú ins gach ród,
Is ó chuala mé do thásg-sa níl Sgáile dhíom beó.

McDonogh is buried in the ancient Dominican Priory in Ballindoon. An inscribed headstone marks the grave. He composed some verses of his own including a satire on his brother Owen who had turned Protestant.

Lament for Terence MacDonough

Brother Owen, if you would speed
To hell, nor heed my opposition ,
Take my sword and chestnut steed-
You need not walk to your Perdition.

A bhráthair Éoin, má táir ag traill
Go teach na bpian tar mo chrois
Beir leat m'arm agus m'each don
Níor chuibhe dhuit dul ann dot chois!

The following verse is attributed to Carolan for Dolly, the niece of Terence Mc Donogh.

Go Craobhaigh choidhce má théidhean tú
Dearc ar mhnaoi na bpéarlaí
Doirionn bhán na maol-rosg,
'S ní baoghal duit an bás.

A young man of the O'Hara's was in love with Dolly but her friends would not allow her to marry him as he had not much wealth. Carolan thought this was a great pity so he composed a song for him. O'Hara learned the song and used to come and sing it often under her window. She eventually eloped with him.

Captain Francis O'Neill has three chapters on harpers, including Carolan, in his music book *Irish Minstrels and Musicians*, chapters vi,vii,and vii.17 His reputation as a writer and collector of numerous valuable books on traditional music is wide spread. His books are Irish Folk Music, a fascinating Hobby, The Music of Ireland, The Dance Music of Ireland, O'Neills Irish Music for Piano or Violin, and Popular selections from the Dance Music of Ireland. During his time in Chicago he preserved the airs, jigs, reels and hornpipes of the ordinary people of Ireland. Even though he was unable to write music his help came from a fellow policeman who hailed from Co. Down, James O'Neill. The following air Máire Dall by Carolan was copied by Captain Francis O'Neill from Forde's Encyclopaedia of Melody and he acknowledges this in his Irish Folk Music. Thomas Davis wrote a poem to this air, and called it Blind Mary. I found it in the 'Spirit of the Nation' (1892). This air by Carolan is also to be found in the Pigot Collection.

We learn from Charles O'Conor's diary (vol.1) that in 1726 his two younger brothers were being taught the harp by a woman harper called Máire Dall. She would have been well known to Carolan and it is said he composed this for her.

Blind Mary by Thomas Davis

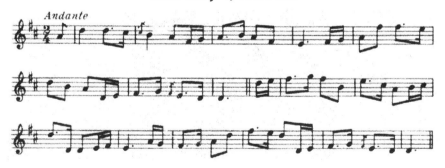

There flows from her spirit such love and delight,
That the face of Blind Mary is radiant with light;
As the gleam from a homestead through darkness will show,
Or the moon glimmer soft through the fast falling snow.

Yet there's a keen sorrow comes o'er her at times,
As an Indian might feel in our northerly climes;
And she talks of the sunset, like parting of friends,
And the starlight as love, that nor changes nor ends.

The Sligo poet Seán O'Gadhra of the O'Gara's of Moy Gara, of the half Barony of Coolavin , Co. Sligo, composed a lament for Carolan in which he says that his music is like rivers of honey and that he was known from Cork to Ceis Corann as the greatest of all the harpers.

Henry and Mary Mac Dermot Roe of Alderford House, Ballyfarnon had five sons and one daughter. Anne who died in 1752, John who turned Protestant, Matthew who became a doctor, Thomas who became Bishop of Ardagh 1747, Charles who married Ellen O'Conor daughter of Denis O'Conor of Belanagare, and Henry who was no comfort to his mother. Henry was engaged to a Miss O'Malley a young lady with a great fortune. His mother and he were on a visit to O'Malleys one day for the wedding date to be arranged. Henry said he needed to visit the O'Donnells of Newport. Carolan was at O'Donnells and they enticed Henry to stay for dinner. The parish priest was there also and while Mary was awaiting her son's return Henry was married before morning to Anne O'Donnell. It was a heavy blow as the girl had no fortune. His patroness outlawed Carolan for some time but all was forgiven eventually.[5]

Dr John Hart, Bishop of Achonry is the subject of at least one tune by Carolan. He and his brother Charles owned Cloonamahon, Collooney, Co. Sligo. To ensure continued ownership they transferred the title to a Protestant friend called Betteridge. Betteridge however registered the property in his own name, took it over and evicted his old friends. The tune "Dr. Hart" was noted by Bunting from Hugh O'Higgins in Co. Mayo.

Dr. John Hart, Bishop of Achonry

Bhéara mé anois an chuairt so gan bhréig,
Mar bhfuil an sagart geanamhuil d'uaisle árd, Gaodhal,
Fear Bréagh íoghmhar tapuidhe,
Fear a ríaradh gastruidhe,
Ar Sheaghan Ó h-Airt go ceart a labhrain-se féin:
Fear don aicme scapadh fíon go réidh,
Is d'olfadh go fras le mac 'a gceoil is a léighin;
Dá mbéinn san Róimh ar bh'ait liom,
Is bíodh mo roghain ionghlactha,
Is cinnte go ndéanfainn easbog mór duit féin.

Charles O' Conor the eldest son of Denis was born in 1710 in Kilmactranny. He was educated by a Franciscan Friar of Creevelea Abbey, Dromahaire, Co. Leitrim. Charles was renowned as a distinguished scholar and historian. He was an excellent performer on the harp.

On visiting the home of Denis O'Conor on Christmas Day 1723, this song was sung by Carolan to the accompaniment of the harp. [6]

Denis O'Conor

M.O.C. N-5

John O'Conor

John O'Connor was one of the O'Connors of Offaly. The tune was used in William Shield's Opera 'The Poor Soldier' in 1782. Blind Billy O'Malley was the Louisborough piper who supplied Patrick Lynch with a copy of the words.

Lady Dillon of Lough Glynn, Co. Roscommon married the 9th Viscount in 1720. She died on the 16th July 1779 in her eighty-ninth year. About the year 1800 the Dillons became absentee landlords. At the end of that century the house and part of the estate was taken over by the Franciscan Missionaries of Mary. It is now a nursing home for senior citizens.

Lady Dillon

The words of "Failte romhad go Kingsland" were obtained from Richard Barrett, of Corn, Belmullett Co. Mayo. For me, this is a major discovery - the connection between one of the West Mayo poets and Carolan. The air was noted from the harp playing of Charles Beirne, one of the competitors at the Belfast Festival in 1792. The song celebrates the marriage of John Drury to Elizabeth Goldsmith, a first cousin of the poet Oliver Goldsmith. Kingsland lies between Boyle and Lough Gara, a few miles from Belanagare.

Fáilte romhad go Kingsland,
A bhinn–bhean na méar lag,
A Phlanda an chúil Chraobhaigh
Le a mbéidh an tír sásta.
Sa tsláinte iad. Is ró bhreagh na sgéala
Mar pósadh le chéile
An lánamhain óg aerach
Bheir pléasur dá gcáirdibh.
Seón Óg mhac Éadbhard
Is a sheód mar chéile
Is go gcumhdaighe Dia saoghalach
Saoilidh lucht saidhbhris
An t saoghal seo le chéile.

(WELCOME TO KINGSLAND.)

TITLE: *MS.: Faulte goh Kingsland or Plangsty Kingsland.*

"Welcome to Kingsland, lady with the small fingers and branching hair! The marriage of the young couple is good news for their friends. May God bless John, son of Edward Drury and his sweet wife. Rich people think there is no pleasure but that of possessing riches. But I would advise them to act like the goodman of old, and marry for pleasure not for profit."

Joseph Cooper Walker (1761-1810) whose manuscripts are in the Royal Irish Academy states that Carolan married Mary McGuire and that they settled on a small farm near Mohill in Co. Leitrim. They are reputed to have had six daughters and one son. One of the most beautiful of his compositions is the love song addressed to Mary, his future partner. Thomas Furlong translated it.

Máire Maguidhir

Mo léun 's mo chradh gan mé 's mo ghrádh,
A ngleanntán áluinn sléibhe
Gan neach d'ár gcáirde bheith le fághail
'N áit ar bith 'n ár ngaobhar ann:
Rígh na ngrás, cá nídh dhamh tháchtadh ort
A chiúib – bhean náireach, bhéusach?
'S gur b'é do ghrádh tá tré mo lár
'Na shaíghiottaibh chráidhte, ghéura!
Is moc ar maidin, do ghluaiseas an ainfhir,
Agus à cúilín ag casadh léithi,
Mar rósá drithléan tá scéimh an leinbh,
Ar gach ball diag teachd le chéile;
A taébh mar an g-criosdal, a bhéilín méala.
Dar liom budh bhinne 'na guth téuda,
Séimh a Leaca, a bhághaid mar an eala,
A's agruadh air dath na g-caor-chan.

Mary Maguire

h! That my love and I
From life's crowded haunts could fly
To some deep shady vale by the mountain,
Where no sound might make it's way,
Save the thrush's lively lay,
And the murmur of the
clear flowing fountain
Where no stranger should intrude
On our hallow'd solitude,
Where no kinsman's cold glance could annoy us.

Where peace and joy might shed
Blended blessings o'er our bed,
And Love! Love alone still employs us.
Still sweet maiden may I see,
That I vainly talk of thee,
In vain in lost love I lie pining,
Úcán úl may worship from afar,
That o'er my dull pathways
The beauty- beaming star, keep shining.

The year of Mary's death is 1733. The following is the last verse of Carolan's elegy for her.

Fuair me seal in Éirinn go haerach is go sóghamhuil
Ag ól le gach tréinfhear bhí éifeachtach ceólmhar
Fágadh 'na ndéidh sin leam féin mé go brónach
I ndeireadh mo shaoghail 's gan mo chéile bheith beó agam.

I spent a space in Ireland happily and in content,
Drinking with every effective hero who was a lover of music,
When they had gone I was left solitary and sorrowful,
At the end of my days with my partner no longer alive.[7]

CHAPTER 6

CAROLAN II - PATRONS

Carolan was welcomed at all the great houses and two of these were in the parish of Kilvarnet; Annaghmore or Nympsfield as it was then called, and Templehouse. Situated in a scenic spot, with Sliabh Gamh to the north and the beautiful hills of Keash, Knocknashee, and Mucklety to the south these houses are in the middle of wild and romantic scenery.[1]

The O'Hara family live at Annaghmore and with the Owenmore river running through the demesne, with rare plants, shrubs and trees, and, rows of magnificent beeches it is breathtaking even today. The O'Haras owned ninety thousand acres down to the seventeenth century. They are one of the most distinguished families in Ireland.[2] After the restoration in 1660, they lost their lands to Edward Cooper(Lord Collooney). Kean O'Hara (Cian) to save his own ancestral home and property was forced to adopt the religion of the invader.

In the fourteenth century, the sept was divided into two divisions, the O'Hara Buidhe of Coolaney and the O'Hara Reagh of Ballyhara. Cian Óg was head of the O'Hara Buidhe in the time of Carolan.[3] His eldest son Charles, (1706-1776) was also a patron of Carolan. Charles sat in the Irish Parliament and corresponded with the great Edmund Burke who was also Irish and an M.P. and the greatest orator of the eighteenth century.

There was a special bond between Charles O'Hara and Edmund Burke. They corresponded over many years. They both belonged to a suspect category – Old Catholic gentry conforming to the Established Church. O'Hara often advised Burke to be cool about political matters. Burke's family had lost all their possessions in Cork. Their letters to each other were coded.[4]

Carolan composed three airs for Cian (Kean) O'Hara. Although Charles was also a patron there is no tune to be had for him today. The O'Haras gave a home to Dr. John Hart and his brother when they were ousted from their home and lands at Cloonamahon during the penal laws. [5]

Charles was one of the incorruptibles who stood steadfast by Henry Grattan. When bribery and titles were flying around, and when he could have made himself Lord

Annaghmore, he remained firm to the end in opposition to the Union.

Tradition has always maintained that the monastery at Benada Abbey owed its origin to the O'Haras [6] whose lands stretched to the river Moy. O'Hara Dubh in 1439 resigned his lordship to his brother Cormac and entered the monastery at Benada. Patrick Lynch (mentioned in a later chapter) noted these words of 'Kean O'Hara' from William Bartley of Killargy, Co. Leitrim.

Kean O'Hara.

Dá mbéinn thiar in Árainn, nó ligCairlinn na séad
Mar ngluaiseann gach sár-long le clairead is le Méad,
B 'fhearr liom gan amhras mar sásadh dom féin
Cupán geal Uí Eagra bheith láimh le mo bhéal.

Were I blessed in sweet Aran or Carlingford shade,
Where ships swiftly sailing with claret and mead,
Diffusing soft pleasure and glee to each heart
Still the cup of O'Hara would greater impart.

One of Kean's neighbours was John Harloe of Rathmullen. He was a man of English stock, and a gentleman of good fortune and fond of amusement. He erected a "Sporting Lodge" at Templehouse and the principal gentry of the county spent quite a lot of their time there. Carolan composed the following verse for Harloe.

Bhí mé lá Marta ar shráid an Droihid Mhóir
Cia casfaidh orm an lá sin ach Seón Hárló
Thug sé buidéil do fhíon dham lár in mo dhorn,
Is nárbh fhurus dham a rádh an lá sin go mbfhearr é ná Cian Óg!

On a March day when standing on Droihidmore's street,
Along with John Harloe I happened to meet;
Spanish wine he did give me -- a full bottle I ween,
So I readily praised him more highly than Kean!

According to Hardiman Kean was furious so Carolan wrote another verse.

Bhí mé lá breágh i dtigh an tabhairne ag ól ,
Tháinig misge mhór sganrach orm is rámhaillighe mhór;
Is truagh nach glas plátaí fáisgthe ar mo sgóig
Nuair a chuir mé Seón Hárló chomh h-árd le Cian Óg!

One fine day in an ale house I happened to sit,
I got fearfully drunk and was raving a bit;
It's a pity my gullet was'nt throttled right clean
When I rated young Harloe as high as young Kean!

Harloe's sister married William Phibbs of Rathmullen and she had twenty-one children. Shane was of Cromwellian stock and got parcels of land in the Ballymote area. He married but had no family.

The Coopers of Markree Castle and the Croftons and Percevals of Templehouse

Templehouse is a Georgian mansion situated on a 1,200-acre estate, overlooking a Knights Templar thirteenth century lakeside castle.[7] There were eleven Norman farmsteads along the Owenmore River at one time. After the suppression of the Templars, the Knights Hospitallers built the stone vaulted rooms on the ground floor in 1320. The property was granted to George Goodman a Co. Meath grazier in 1580. His nephew William Crofton built the moated brick house in 1627. The Percevals have lived at Temple House since 1664, when George Perceval married Mary Crofton. William Crofton was given the office of the First Fruits and of the twentieth Parts and received the sum of £86/13/4. In 1617 he was appointed Auditor General for Connacht and Ulster.

Templehouse was restored in 1825. At this stage George Perceval was made Register of the Prerogative Court. Mrs Jane Perceval died of famine fever in 1847 while tending to the tenants in their dire need. Her eldest son sold Templehouse in 1859, and under the Encumbered Estates Act it was purchased by an English man called Hall-Dare who evicted so many of the tenants that the agent L'Estrange asked the third Perceval son to return from Hong Kong and buy the estate back. This he did in 1863 and rebuilt and refurbished it the following year. At the same time he brought back many families from Ireland, England and America. He rebuilt their homes and put them back on their lands.

In 1722 John Perceval married Nancy Cooper of Markree Castle. O'Carolan composed a lovely air for her. It was noted by Bunting from Paddy Quinn near Armagh. It had also been noted by Patrick Lynch from James Dowd a farmer from Screen in Tireragh. Edward Cooper, a Cornet in Richard Collooney's regiment of dragoons, founded the Cooper family in Ireland. Having settled in Sligo, he became the owner of a large estate. His son Arthur, of Markee Castle, Co. Sligo, had two sons and five daughters.

*17. Nancy Cooper. *Second Air*

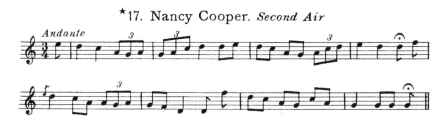

Nancy Cooper

Is fíor dheas a ghnaoidh ghlan is a píob gheal
Le'r claoideadh na mílte fear;
Scannraigh sí gach scéimh, cúl cas na gcraobh,
Is dlúith geal a déad, an cheansach chiúin.
Is mín, milis, maiseach, mánla,
Socair, cráfach, gan gruaim, do ghnúis , a bhean,
Do shúil ghlas, do leaca is áille, sud na táinte aici mar spré.

Pigott and Forde also got this tune from Hugh O'Beirne. Markree Castle is still owned by the Coopers. It is situated in the Tirerill part of the parish of Ballisadare. Markree demesne is one of the finest in the country. It is well watered by the Unsin river. A belt of trees goes all around the demesne; oak, ash, beech, lime, elm, chestnut, sycamore, and some white thorn. It appears as a Castle on the Down Survey maps of the seventeenth century. It has undergone many alterations and restorations. The Markree Observatory was founded in 1832. Some of the most distinguished astronomers have been in charge there.

The Croftons of Longford House in the Barony of Tireragh

The territory of Tireragh belonged to the ancient Irish clann of the O'Dowds. They were a maritime people. After varying fortunes the family were still holding positions of importance down to 1603, when they were pardoned by King James 1. By 1649 the properties of all the old landowners of Tireragh were confiscated by the Commonwealth, and given to Cromwell's officers and soldiers. This we presume is how Henry Crofton got Longford House, Beltra.[8]

Longphort, one of the chief seats of the O'Dowds was distinguished as Longphort Úi Dhubhda. Duald McFirbish the great genealogist who wrote in 1660 says in his Genealogy of the Hy Fiachra ' that the English erected all the bawn or fortress of Longphort except Leaba an Eich-bhuide, which was erected by Brian O'Dowd.[9] The Barony of Tireragh lies along the north-western coast of Co. Sligo. A poem called The *O'Dowds of Tireragh* was obtained from James O'Dowd of Skreen by Patrick Lynch in 1802.

Uí Dhúda Thir Fhéachrach

Cumdach Mhic Dé ar a'gcliar-chloinn deagh- mhúinte,
Cuideachta na féile nárbh 'fhéidir a dhiúltadh!
Níorbh úirse an t-éideadh gan bréig a gcine Iúdaigh
Nó thuas os cionn Gaodhalaibh clann tréigheach Uí Dhúda.

Ní deise an Bealtaine Fá na bláthann' bréagh úire
'S na soillgighe maidin Shamhraid nó deallra a nguise-
Fir cróga calma, tá ceannasach ciallmhar,
Dia dtigeach fiadh an ghleanna go talamh Thír Fhéachrach,
Níor bha leis féin a bheanna ó mharcachan éich riabaigh!

Tráth ghluaiseas sí' un siúibhail, do choiscéim glan éadtrom
Caitilín Ní Dhúda, lamh clúite na féile,
Ainnir na maon-rosg, na gcúrcan bréagh péarlach,
Beidh fiadh leis an túr-fhlaith, nó cúpla má's fíor!

The O'Dowds of Tireragh

May the Son of God protect the noble, musical family,
The household of all-compelling hospitality!
Truly the Levites were not ranked higher among the Jews
Than the virtuous O'Dowds above the Gaels.

May, with its pretty fresh flowers, is not more beautiful ,
A summer morning is not brighter, than the glory of their faces—
The valiant brave men, powerful and famous;
Dearly I love then, the O'Dowd family.

When they go out hunting of a morning,
Valiant and brave mighty and wise.
If the stag of the valley came to Tireragh,
The rider of the dapple-grey would not let him keep his antlers.

And when she walks out with neat, light footstep,
Kathleen O'Dowd, renowned for hospitality
With her modest eye,and her fine gleaming curls
She will get a stag,or two if she can.

Longford House was burned down during the 1914-1918 war. A native of the district told us that the ground floor was covered with moss to be dried out. It was then packed and sent to the war headquarters in London. The dried moss was used in the making of bandages and sent out to the front. However Longford House went up in flames when the moss caught fire from a lighted candle. A new house was built at the back of the Castle.

The history of the Croftons who came to Ireland in Elizabethan times was written by Henry Thomas Crofton in York 1911.[10] Thomas Crofton of Mote Co. Roscommon was created First Baronet in 1661. The Sligo Croftons were Catholics. Edward Crofton was a Justice of the Peace for Sligo. He had a large family, fifteen in all. James his third son fell in love with a Protestant and both her father and his, opposed the match. James turned Protestant and obtained the family estates which was the custom in Penal times. He died in 1775. His grandson Sir James Crofton became the first Baronet of Longford House.

In January 1671 the great scholar Dubhaltach MacFirbish was murdered at Doonflyn, west of the village of Skreen, Co. Sligo by one Thomas Crofton. According to the historian Nollaig O'Muraile, Dubhaltach who was over eighty at the time probably had made some slighting remark which angered Crofton where upon

Crofton drew a knife and stabbed the elderly scholar. The Croftons were deeply ashamed of the terrible act committed by one of their members.[11]

Carolan composed at least four pieces for the Croftons. Bunting noted the tunes for the Crofton family from Charles Fanning who perfomed at the Belfast Harp Festival in 1792. Incidentally Arthur O'Neill the famous harper visited Longford House in 1786.

Miss Crofton

Tanrego House was the home of the Irwin family from the mid seventeenth century, to the early eighteenth century. The main avenue to the house was blocked with fallen trees from the bad storm of November 1999.

59. Colonel John Irwin

Raca mé ar cuairt suas gan spás
Fá dhéin duine uasail suadhamhail sásta,
An Coirnéal suairc tá ar bhruach na trágha,
Scéal dob áil liomt trácht air.
Fear nachleigionn sgíth don chupan,
Is anmhail leis Ceól agus ól gan racán,
An t-óigfear Ghaodhalac Gállda.
'Sé seo Seón gan amhras

We will take our way without delay, to see a Noble, brave and gay,
The Gallant Colonel near the sea, him I mean to treat of
With mirth and joy he fills his glasses,
Delights to cheer both lads and lasses
This is John I will answer the brave English Irelánder.

We presume the song was composed not long after the peace of Utrecht in 1713, when Colonel Irwin was home from the wars.[12] He was High Sheriff of Sligo in 1731. He was later visited by Arthur O'Neill. The history of the Irwin family shows that in 1665 Henry Irwin got a grant of land under the Cromwellian settlement.[13] Alexander also got a grant of land in lieu of arrears of pay owed to him. They were near neighbours of the Croftons of Longford House. One of the Croftons was married to a daughter of O'Conor Don. The Croftons though Catholics gave the Irwin family shelter and concealment from the Jacobite forces. The house is still in good condition. [14]

Jones of Benada Abbey, Ardneglasse, Ardnaree, Bellaghy and Sligo town

In the sixteenth century the army played an important part in the Government of Co. Sligo. It made connections between families and pointed to areas where they might settle. Roger Jones among others had first been employed as an Elizabethan soldier.[15] He was one of three constables in charge of a small garrison. Jones served in the army in Ireland in the 1590's as a lieutenant. In 1607 he was appointed constable of the new jail there. At this time he had no landed estate. But by 1616 he had property in and around Sligo town and at Benada Abbey. By 1635 he was one of the top landlords in the county. He leased land at Rosses Point from the Bishop of Elphin. He had many connections by marriage. His son married the daughter of Henry Hart of Doocastle. Other members married into the O'Hara family of Annaghmore. Alicia married Roebuch Crean of Sligo. Jones was knighted in 1624. One of the Jones married a daughter of O'Conor Don.

The first land settlement after the Restoration brought Jeremy Jones 4,000 acres to his holding. Roger Jones was the first provost of Sligo town. He traded in wool and other goods. As time went on the name of Jones was well known throughout Sligo. In Ardnaglass in the parish of Skreen a patent to hold two fairs was granted to Loftus Jones after Rory Mac Sweeney was dispossessed. By 1828 The Sligo Liberal and Independent Club was formed and among the members was Daniel Jones of Banada. St. John's Church was built by Sir Roger Jones and in his will he says ' My body I commit to the earth, in my toombe in the chappel I lately erected in the parish of St. John's in Sligo.[16]

The following tune composed by Carolan for John Jones was noted by Bunting from Denis Hempson, the oldest of all the harpers at the Belfast Harp Festival. According to Hardiman, the Galway historian John Jones was descended from Jeremy Jones of Ardneglasse and Bellaghy in Co. Sligo. However the Mundy O'Reilly MS., p99 in the

Royal Irish Academy says that this song was composed by Carolan for Captain Jones of Tireragh, who was in love with a young lady and was afraid to propose in case her parents would refuse. Loftus Jones is another of Carolan's songs noted by Bunting from Charles Fanning. He was the son of Thomas and Susanna Jones of Ardnaglass, Co. Sligo.

John Jones

A óig-bhean mhín, fóir orm déan,
Fóill! Ná saoil m'fhógairt ón tsaoghal.
Is leór duit mar taoim creapailte ag an mbás,
Gointe, greadtaí ó do Shaighdibh grádha.
Má rinne tú an fheall 's nach dtiocfa tú liom
Mar dubhrais ar maidin síos faoi an nghleann,
Mo sgaoith bhuan mhallacht sgaoilim leatsa,
Mí ní mhairfead- is me Seon Jones.

This is only one of three tunes Carolan composed for the Jones family. As the years passed the family expanded and lived in various parts in Sligo. In 1858 under The Encumbered Estates Court, the property of Benada was made over to Mother Mary Aikenhead founder of the Sisters of Charity.[17] The remaining Jones's were all in religion. Daniel married Maria the sister of Joseph Mór McDonnell of Doocastle in 1816. They had six children, three boys and three girls. Two boys entered the Jesuits. Two girls became Sisters of Charity and the third became a sister of Mercy in Elphin. The third boy, Freddie, wanted to become a Jesuit but he died of consumption and was buried in the little family graveyard.

Miss MacDermot or The Princess Royal
This beautiful air was composed by Turlough O'Carolan for Mary the daughter of Hugh MacDermot the second son of Cathal Roe MacDermot who died in 1694. Hugh was the first MacDermot of Shruffe and Coolavin. Mary his daughter married Owen O'Rourke who lived at Tarmon on the western shore of Lough Allen. He was the last of the O'Rourkes to have a position of importance in Co. Leitrim. He was born in 1670 and died in 1728. They did not have a family.

Miss MacDermot

The origin of The Mac Dermots can be traced to the fifth century. Their dwelling place in 1184 was the Rock of Lough Cé. They eventually became Kings of Moylurg. The ancient name for Moylurg was Magh Luirg an Dagda, a name connected with the legendary Tuatha de Danann.

Síochán ar dtús ort, a chúl chas na gcraobh,
A phlannda don árd-fhuil ón gcuan sin Loch Cé;
Níl cuan, níl caltha, níl áit ar bith ina dtéidhim
Nach é chluinim ag a' ngasraid gurabh í Máillí a rug a' chraobh.

By her marriage to Owen O'Rourke, Mary MacDermot united two historic families. Mary was displeased with O'Carolan for not mentioning her in his composition for her husband during his lifetime. O'Carolan then composed Máire an Chúil fhinn and this appeased her feelings.

In 1617 Brian MacDermot received from King James I the grant of his ancestral lands. The original of the grant to Brian is at Coolavin. It is known in the family as the Title Deeds of Rockingham. Rockingham was the name given to the estate when Charles II gave the same lands to the King family. Pre-Cromwellian settlers in Co. Roscommon were the Kings of Boyle. They did not move to Rockingham until the early eighteenth century.[18]

From 1707 the new home of the Mac Dermots was in the townland of Shroofe on the slopes of Mullachatee beside Lough Gara. Rockingham became the seat of Viscount Lord Lorton over two hundred years ago.The MacDermots still live at Coolavin and are highly regarded by all. They and the O'Conors of Cloonalis are the last of the Gaelic Chieftains.

Rockingham, the Seat of Viscount Lorton

CHAPTER 7

DANCE TUNES OF THE WEST OF IRELAND

The following two jigs are as old as the hills!

The Connachtmans Rambles and Farewell to Gurteen

The Connachtmans Rambles has been played at my home as far back as I can remember. *Farewell to Gurteen* I picked up from local musicians as Gurteen is only six miles from my home. It was played for all who had to emigrate and bid farewell to that lovely area.

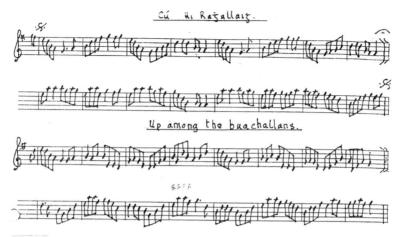

Two reels when played well brought everyone to their feet for the Lancers or the Eight Hand set. The first one "Ó'Raghallaigh's Hound" is part of the collection of Art McMorrow in Collooney in Co. Sligo. Art gave this first tune to Dan Healy along with many others. (It is also in Ó'Neill's Collection).[1] Art's father was the well-known Sligo piper, Seán Mac Morrow. A manuscript copy of *A Sligo Piper*, 1884-1949 was presented to Art Mac Morrow's family by Martin Power who put the MS. together. The second reel "Up Among the Buachallans" is also called "Batt Henry's". Both these reels were played with great feeling in Sligo, North Roscommon and Mayo. Batt Henry was a schoolteacher in the primary school in Emlaughton, Ballymote. He played well and taught the fiddle. He was the grandfather of Dermot Henry who emigrated to the USA and is a well known singer out there. Another man who went to the States some years ago from Leitrim is Vincent Harrison. He became friendly with the late Martin Wynne and Dick O'Beirne and they played the best of traditional music every chance they got. Vincent said Martin often spoke of two Ballymote musicians of the 1890s, Cipín Scanlon and Mattie Killoran. Cipín had spent some time in Scotland and loved to play Phil O'Beirnes Delight. Martin said he often went home from sessions heartbroken after listening to these two great fiddlers and aching to learn their tunes.

The following three polkas were played for the last round of the Lancers. We had no name for them. When I came to live in Dublin and visited St. Mary's Music Club with Eileen Boyle, John Egan from Sooey, Ballintogher in Sligo was in charge. He was very special and everyone loved him. Even though it was called St. Mary's Music Club we all knew it as John Egans. These polkas were his favourites so that they became known as John Egan's Polkas. He played a concert flute. The club was above Lavin's pub in Church Street. John arrived every Wednesday evening with a little bag of turf on the carrier. He was there first and had a fire lighting before anyone came. When the music

began the strains wafted down to the Four Courts. Before a tune was played John raised his hand and said "Remember now everybody, take it easy like the man going to the bog".

George Rowley (Department of Education and Science) whose late father never failed to attend the club told me these musicians met in each others houses for quite a while. As children were hard to get to sleep at night, Mrs. Rowley suggested they rent a place to meet in. This they did and everyone was happy. Mrs Rowley baked for them all as they played on Sunday mornings in her house. Her husband was a good singer and composed many songs. Ciarán Mac Mathuna made a collection of them some years ago. George spoke of musicians Paddy White, Tony Mc Mahon, John Kelly, Joe Ryan, Eugene McGlynn and Tommy Peebles. Hughie Mc Cormack, a Leitrim man who had spent time in the Curragh and became fluent in Irish with the help of Máirtín Ó'Cadhain, played the fiddle and entertained all with great stories. He played in later years in Donoghues. Tommy Potts, fiddle, Tommy Reck, uilleann pipes, Vincent Broderick flute, Jim Masterson, accordeon and Declan Masterson, uilleann pipes also played in the club.

Musicians called into Lavins when they came to Dublin, among them Paddy Taylor from England, and Larry Reddigan from the USA. Tommy Flynn from Lough Arrow on the fiddle was a welcome guest. We visited him three weeks before his death and he played some of Coleman's tunes. He had a visitors' book which was between four to six inches thick in A 4 size and every square inch was full of names of those who visited him. Dan Healy and I may have been the last to sign it. I sincerely hope it will be taken to the Archives. Another regular visitor to Lavins was Frank Harte the great singer whose father came from Ballindoon. Jimmy Joe Mc Kiernan, a good fiddle player came to the club whenever he was up from Leitrim.

There were many, many more who came to St. Mary's Music Club including Antoinette, Mary, Martha and Brigid Bergin, Gerry Byrne, Eamon Lane, Louis and Vincent Collins. Dick Hogan sang some of his good old songs. Pierce Greegan came from Loughlinstown on occasions. He played the war pipes but not in the club. Here he played the whistle. But he always led the Oireachtas Céilí in the Mansion House with the war pipes and in full Irish Kilt. He also was member of a club in Ely Place where the Irish language and Irish music were promoted. One never knew who or how many would turn up to John Egan's Club (St.Mary's.)

Those were wonderful nights, in the fifties and the sixties. The company was good. John's lovely daughters were there. John Clarke was there every night. He was too old now to play the pipes but he still made reeds and put many youngsters right about how music should be played. Bill Davis, another veteran who loved the music also attended. Maggie and Peter Flynn came to listen. Peter was a good piper but was too old to play. They regaled the audience with their stories of great sessions. One of Maggie's stories is worth a repeat. It was never confirmed as being true. The members of St. Mary's club decided to go on an outing to Ireland's Eye. They got on the boat and as it was a fine day they played music until they reached the island. They all enjoyed the outing and prepared to go back. When they got into the boat Tom Mulligan sat on Jim Seery's fiddle by mistake. It was the end of a beautiful friendship and the beginning of the strengthening of the Piper's Club.

The Brophys

Pat Brophy the piper from Tipperary (and living in Crumlin) and many of his sons, Mick on pipes, Tom on accordion, Brendan on drums, Joe on accordion and James were there on different occasions to add to the music. Eileen Boyle played in their band in the late forties. They recorded often for Radio Éireann. The studio in those days was at the top of the General Post Office in O'Connell St. They played at many Céilídhes. Pearl Mc Bride played with them also.

Another who attended St. Mary's Music Club was Des O'Connor, flute and concertina player. His music was very popular. One Christmas Dan Healy was going to the west and was talking to him at the garage on Conyingham Road where he worked. Dessie was in great form. After wishing each other Christmas greetings, Dan set out for the west. On reaching home some few hours later he turned on the news and to his horror he heard of Dessie's death in a road accident. His son is continuing the music tradition and is an excellent performer. Then there was Tom Mulligan and Neil, Eileen Boyle and Liam Rowsome on fiddles. Leo Rowsome played the uilleann pipes and piano accordion. John Egan shook his head right through the tunes, as the pipes were being played, but he always allowed individuals with "strange instruments" to give a recital of a tune or two, and thanked them for their performance.

Tom Murphy played flute, Ciaran Collins whistle, Tommy Potts fiddle and Tommy Reck pipes. Vincie Crehan played whistle and flute. Paddy Bán Ó'Broin played flute and was an old time traditional dancer. It was said he could dance on a six-penny piece. John Brennan played flute and later on in life played the whistle. Brendan Breathnach played uilleann pipes and was an excellent listener. Tom Kearns, Tom Glacken and sons played fiddles. Peter James Mc Gettrick, was very shy and when coaxed to play, performed the Coulin as if he were in the Concert Hall. Paddy Taylor played flute, and when Fred Finn and his sister Tilly arrived with their fiddles there was a great welcome for them, as there was for Paddy O'Brien and Kathleen Smyth.

Tommy Leahy who was quite an elderly gentleman at this time, enjoyed the music and listened carefully to every tune. He was a Kilkenny hurler in his day. He left his fiddle down carefully when he came into the club. Near the end of the night John Egan would stand and say "Now Tommy Leahy will give us The Lark". Reluctantly Tommy stood up and rendered that most beautiful piece of classical music - The Lark in the Clear Air. And of course we were all expecting The Lark in the Morning – A fine old double jig.

As the club became well known, it was the place to be on a Wednesday night and many more started to attend - Seán and James Keane, Des Gerrity, Paddy Maloney, John McNamara, Eoghain and Ciarán Ó'Raghallaigh, Mick O'Connor, Pearl O'Shaughnessy (she now organises the Club) and her sons. Every year brought more musicians as they moved to Dublin to work – Dan Healy on concert flute, Mick and Jack Frain, the O'Grady brothers, Sean Garvey and his sister Ita, Ignatius Keane, Donnchada O'Muineachain and Seán Garvey the sean nós singer, Mick O'Meara, Paddy Masterson, Tony Smyth , Kathleen and Sean Nesbit, Paddy Tracey, John Dwyer and Mick Tubridy. Louis Quinn and Martin Wynne called when they were home from the States. Micháel Allen, Séamus Mac Mathuna and many more played there.

When repairs had to be carried out in the Church Street pub, the club moved to

Brú na Gael, in North Great George's Street. The only spare room was at the top of the house – four stories up. It was all right in summer and no one complained of having to climb the rickety stairs. But in winter the dedication of the players and listeners was so great that they ventured in through hail, snow, rain and frost and climbed those stairs to a cold unheated badly lit room, and the place became alive with joy and love for the music.

In time Brú Na Gael was needed for other things and the club was again without a home. On this occasion Dan Healy was responsible for getting Keogh's in Smithfield (now the Cobblestones established by the Mulligan family.) The next move was to King's Inn in Henrietta Street. The music lovers never failed to support John Egan and his friends. Anyone visiting Dublin got a great welcome. The loneliness for one's home in the country was no more. The club moved to Hughes' pub at the back of the markets in Chancery St. Long may it thrive. Others who were there – Peg Mc Grath R.I.P. Catherine McEvoy, Frank Slockett, and his father-in law Dominick. John Gannon from Moate arrived many times with his father who could play the concertina all night long.

The older generation were dedicated and in no small way this enthusiasm helped the present generation of young capable and efficient students of music. One very popular visitor to the club was Gerard O'Grady who wrote the folk column of the evening papers. He was instrumental in spreading the news for venues of traditional music. He loved the music and was a good singer and a good friend. Ar deis De go raibh a anam.

While John Egan's club was at the top of the house in Brú na Gaedeal, Caitlin Maude had a singers' club downstairs called "An Bonnan Buí ". She insisted that all who came to this club must know the Irish language. She herself was an excellent singer and her club was 'lán go doras' at all times. She brought a 'draíocht ' to the club. Her poetry and ámhraín ar an sean nós' have been recorded by Gael Linn. Her poetry in Irish could not be surpassed. Ireland's loss at her passing is felt everywhere.

Caitlín was born in Rosmuc, in the Connemara Gaeltacht in 1941. She graduated from U.C.G and taught for awhile. ' *Treall*' and '*An Mháthair* 'are two of her best poems. In *Treall* she was dissatisfied with the way the world is going. Her last line of this is "Ach, a Dhia, táim tuirseach". Did she foresee the end before it came? My recollection of Caitlín is - seeing her at a Gaelic meeting in Omeath in 1969 standing side by side with Máirtín Ó' Cadhain, Deasún Breathnach and many more fíor Gaedhaeil speaking for the rights of our native language. They fired those present with enthusiasm. Deasún always spoke Irish and published articles as Gaeilge in the newspapers down through the years. He has written many books and poetry. I met him first at the All Ireland Fleadh Ceoil in Boyle Co. Roscommon, in the early sixties. Later I often saw Caitlin in Club an Chonnradh in Harcourt Street enjoying traditional music. Her death eighteen years ago is still being mourned.

Many musicians came to Dublin from the west and created a niche for themselves. One man who lived in London for many years, a native of Ahascragh, Co. Galway was Máirtín Burns. He returned for the first Fleadh Ceoil in Listowel and became the All-Ireland Champion on the fiddle. The rest of his life he spent in Dublin with many visits to Sean ac' Donnchada a Connamara man who taught all his life in Ahascragh. Seán was a traditional singer and made many records with Gael Linn. These two men were friends for life. Máirtín called him Sean 'The Masther,' (Master) and had a deep respect for him. Máirtín stayed at Seán's home every time he went west. His last journey there was an eventful one for all. He sat in the armchair beside the fire and Bríd (Seán's wife) went out to the kitchen to get him a good hot drink. When she returned Mairtín had gone to his eternal reward in those few short minutes. The year was 1998.

A lovely reel that comes to mind is called Fearghal Ó'Gadhra.[2] It had been named after the historical figure who sponsored the Franciscans who compiled the Annals of the Four Masters in 1636. The O'Garas were Gaelic Chieftains in Co. Sligo in 1641. They had three castles in Coolavin – Moygara, Cuppanagh and Derrymore all overlooking the beautiful lake, Lough Gara. Feargal's father died before he had come of age and his wardship was granted to Sir Theobald Dillon. Feargal was elected MP. for Sligo in 1634. After the rising of 1641 he is on record as having protected a family by the name of Browne, who were being persecuted because of their religion. The Castle of Moygara is on the slopes of Mullach a tSí and is in ruins. Feargal died about 1660.[3]

The Hills of Clogher and The Carracastle Lass

Clogher was part of the O'Gara estate until the middle of the seventeenth century. MacDermots in 1879 bought the estate and house at Clogher. It lies some three miles from Old Coolavin on the opposite side of Monasteraden village on the road to Ballaghaderreen.

The Carracastle Lass is a great favourite in the west. Carracastle is only about six miles from Ballaghaderreen. The mystery of the title was never solved – Who was the Lass? In Dublin it is called - George White's Favourite. Playing these two reels together make a very lively session.[4]

The Battering Ram

The Battering Ram. Large poles of timber were used to batter down houses of those being evicted during the Land War. It is a popular jig at all sessions.

Martin Wynne and Dan Healy

In 1992 Martin Wynne came home from the Bronx to be made Honorary President of Comhaltas Ceoltóirí Éireann. He and Dan Healy were good friends and corresponded often. Martin was a native of Bunninaden and was one of the sweetest players on fiddle. This was his last trip to Ireland. Martin Wynne set sail for the USA. in 1948 and only returned to Ireland for holidays. He would have loved to have met Michael Coleman but as he said himself "Coleman cheated on me by three years twice – he left his native Killavil (the half parish of Buninadden,) three years before I was born, and he went to heaven three years before I arrived in New York". Martin personifies a great tradition that will never die even though he has gone to his eternal reward. His reels no 1 and no 2 are excellent.

CONROY'S NO. 2.   A. CONROY

Here I wish to pay tribute to the late Andy Conroy from Loughglynn Co. Roscommon. He played the uilleann pipes with style and dignity. We never heard enough of his music as for the past years he listened rather than played. His early years were spent working in Dublin, in England and New York. He was related to Johnnie Gorman the famous Roscommon itinerant piper who played in Doocastle and in all the counties around at house dances and fairs. When in Dublin he got instructions from Leo Rowsome. Later he studied the playing of Seamus Ennis, Johnnie Doran and Willie Clancy. It was only when he heard Patsy Tuohy who had the Connacht or tight style of piping that he aimed to do likewise. He practised 'cranning' every chance he got and he became an expert piper. He is buried in his native soil in Loughglynn. (Cranning is the most characteristic ornamentation used on the uilleann pipes and is tight fingering.) [5]

Andy Conroy and John Kelly

Patsy Tuohy was born in Loughrea in 1865 and was brought to the USA by his parents when he was four. It has been said he had no equal anywhere. He learned the pipes from a Mayo man – Bartley Murphy. Both Patsy and Bartley had great command of the regulators. Patsy's expert manipulation of a great set of Taylor pipes made him the centre of attraction. Performing as a comedian and a piper Patsy Tuohy played from place to place in the USA. He always had an engagement.

An excellent fiddle player that is seldom mentioned is Pat Coyle from Ballymote who lived in the first part of the twentieth century. Michael Coleman got tunes from him long before he went to America. Pat's favourite was The Millstone. When his mother died she was buried in the old Abbey Churchyard in Ballymote. In the stillness of the lonely nights the sound of music came from the graveyard. Pat was sitting on his mother's grave playing the fiddle for her.

Monasteraden had a pipe band in the 1930s. It comprised eleven members: three Cryan brothers, Sean Golden from Shroofe, John and Mattie Regan from Fauleens, Ned and Jimmy Flannery. They usually made their appearance on St. Patrick's Day. The band entered the Feis Ceoil at Sligo in the thirties and won first place.

Clogher Hall was a great centre for the local community.[6] Some very good traditional concerts were held. On a particular night in 1933, a selection of local musicians gathered for one of these concerts. Jim Coleman a brother of Michael's was to lead the music. But he arrived without a fiddle and the consternation was great. It appears his wife Maenie burned his fiddle when he refused to go to the bog. She had put it at the back of the fire because there was nothing else to burn! It was well known that Jim was not fond of work. Often he set out to play at a house dance on the donkey and cart, stayed all night and slept in the cart on the way home and the donkey always knew his way. But this time the day was saved as Madam MacDermot got her daughter Ruth to lend him her own fiddle. With a look of amazement on his face Jim faced the audience in a world of his own. His helpers were John Drury and Eugene Giblin who were cousins and played concert flutes and Jim Donoghue played the tin whistle. John Drury was definitely a professional. I remember him in the late forties but like most of the young men of those days he had to emigrate. Patsy McHugh had great memories of rambling musicians. One was Johnny Gorman the piper. There were great house dances when he visited Monasteraden.[7] Before Michael Coleman went to America, he, Johnny Gorman and Jim Coleman played one night in 1905 in Monasteraden. People talked of this great night for years. Lady de Freyne heard him play at a crossroads dance near Frenchpark and she thought he was very good. So she made him a present of a very good set of pipes, Shortly after this he got first prize at the Oireachtas in Dublin in 1902. Gorman fell on hard times and was drowned in 1917.

The hornpipe is of English origin and comes down from about 1760. The Irish have adopted it as their own. It has a structure not unlike that of the reel but there is an emphasis on the third part of each bar. *The Flower of Edinburgh* and *The Galway Hornpipe* were played for one part of the set dance.

The Flower of Edinburgh

The Galway Hornpipe

The Lark in the Morning is No. 240 in O'Neill's book. It is a special rare jig of ancient lineage and possesses an individuality all of its own. James Carbury, a native of Quebec, living in Chicago had picked up quite a few tunes from an old Kerry fiddler named Courtney while he was living in Canada. Carbury recorded the tunes on an Edison phonograph, and it was eventually transmitted to Ó'Neill's note book as *The Lark in the Morning.*

The Lark in the Morning

The Glenview Céilí Band, formed in the fifties won the McCarthy Cup three times at the Feis Ceoil in Sligo, in the early sixties. They had engagements in all the towns of Mayo and Sligo. On St. Stephen's Day and St. Patrick's Day they travelled to ceilithe in Ceathru Thaidhg in the Erris peninsula, Co. Mayo. They played the best of traditional music but unfortunately there were no recordings made in the west at that time.

Living in Dublin in the early sixties it was exciting to read in the daily newspapers of the setting up of a County Board for Traditional music. I had heard of the Pipers Club but had not been there. Their meetings were held in Árus Ceannt in Thomas Street. This was called after Éamonn Ceannt one of the seven signatories executed in 1916. Éamonn worked in the Dublin Corporation and was a member of Connradh na Gaeilge. He was a fine piper and was one of those who founded the Pipers Club in 1900. He was the secretary. He won first prize twice at the Oireachtas. Éamonn stood for the rights of women and for the strikers in Dublin in 1913. Before his death he said "I wish to record the gallantry and fearless calm determination of the men who fought with me". He had a special interest in sean-nós and he prepared rooms in the Pipers Club for classes. He was executed on the 8 May, 1916.

After the death of Éamonn Ceannt the club became defunct until 1926. It was an effort to continue. Some of the members collected money on the streets to enable the club to go ahead - like Tom Rowsome, John Potts and Tommy Reck. In the Liberties area of Old Dublin, there was a thriving folk music tradition. So the club in Thomas Street Club became a meeting place for country folk and city folk alike. Classes were started. Céilí Bands held practices there. It was a hub of activity every Saturday night. Eventually the founding of Comhaltas Ceoltóirí Éireann in 1951 brought change. The Pipers Club continued to retain "a special position" for some years and eventually a headquarters was purchased in Monkstown.

Another club continued in Bridgefoot Street. Here the Clare People and their friends held sessions every Thursday night. The Clare sets were danced and the older people taught the nyouth. Here Willie Clancy came when he was in town. The talk at the time was how like Patsy Tuohy he played. Seán Keane's father and mother were there. Both were very good fiddlers. Mary Bergin, Brigid, Martha and Antoinette, her sisters were there and Antóin Mac Gabhan with his fiddle and many dancers. Josie Murphy from Clare was in charge of the club and Antóin married her niece. Two other Clare men always there were Mick McGwann and Siney Crotty. Mick lived with an uncle on the next road to us and often dropped in. In those days the key was left in the door all night. It was the way times were and there were no robbers. One Sunday morning I awoke to the beautiful sound of an Irish air. I crept downstairs to find Mick sitting on the armchair beside a blazing turf fire playing away to his heart's content. He knew the key was always in our door. The Clare Street club was an exciting place to visit and was sorely missed when the place was demolished. There were many concerts in Guinness's Hall off Thomas Street and here Frank Harte sang his wonderful songs. Willie Clancy often came and charmed the audience.

The Eamonn Ceannt band played at Céilídhe's throughout the country and made many broadcasts. A long-playing record was made by the band and it is interesting to know it is still played for teaching Irish dancing.

The Eamonn Ceannt band

Mrs. Nora O'Gara was one of the all time 'great musicians' and a contemporary of Michael Coleman. Back in 1940 she took part with Margaret Horan and Dick Brennan in a Feis which was held at Killavil. Nora had been the musical partner of Jim Coleman for almost thirty years. In the fifties she gave many fine performances at the old Céilí House at Killavil.[8] One night at a concert Fr. O'Hara introduced her on stage, as " the great living link with the past, the woman who played with Michael Coleman." Her son John who plays the fiddle survives her.

Fred Finn was born in Killavil in 1919 and died in 1986. He was rich in musical tradition and toured the U.S.A. with the Coleman Country Céilí Band in 1972. He was a witty jovial happy man and it was a pleasure to be in his company as he regaled all around him with his stories. Fred Finn's reel is played in all parts of the country.

John Brennan was born on the 20th October 1898. His wife Josie came from Croagh and attended Killavil National school. John played football for Sligo and played in goals with the great 1923 junior team. He later played with the 1928 senior team in Croke Park.

Ed Reavy, a Cavan man left Ireland in 1912 and settled in Philadelphia. He was a renowned fiddle player. Actually it was said that 'he could make the fiddle talk.' He equalled Michael Coleman in his talent for traditional music. He composed many tunes and his books can be found in bookshops throughout the country.

Reel Of Mullinavat

Dan Healy and Ciarán Ó'Raghallaigh

CHAPTER 8

PATRICK LYNCH'S COLLECTION FOR BUNTING IN CO. MAYO AND THE WEST MAYO POETS

Seán Gairbhí, Caitlín Seighin, Dónal Ó'hÉalaí, Máire Gairbhí agus Paddy Fitz

The 2000 St. Patrick's Day Festival, called 'An tEarrach Thiar', in Gaoth Sáile in north west Mayo was a unique occasion. Teach Iorrais is a real haven. It stands amidst the rugged landscape of the Mullet Peninsula. From here one can view the Atlantic Ocean and the Nephin mór and Nephin beag mountains. Gaoth Sáile (meaning The Salty Wind) is in the Erris peninsula. Here John Millington Synge visited and got inspiration to write "The Playboy of the Western World." The strand where the races were held in the play still has races there each year.

Eagle Island, Belmullet

Muintearas Mhaigh Eo and Radio na Gaeltachta were there in full strength. People came from the Glens of Antrim, Dundalk, Sligo, Roscommon, all parts of Mayo and Dublin. Music played by children enchanted the adults and sessions went on until the early hours of the morning. Jim Deane and his son on the button accordion and his daughter on the concert flute, with Joe Carey on the accordion, Dan Healy on concert flute, Paddy Mills on fiddle, all played with 'fuinneamh'. Treasa Ní Ghearraigh and Vincent McGrath, with their CDRom on Dún Chaocháin were there. It was an unforgettable weekend. Seán Ó'Coistealbha and family, Séan Ó'hÉalaithe, Micheal and Caitlín Ó Seighin, Máirtín Davi O Coistealbha to name only a few added to the success of the weekend. Justin Salmon and Séan Garvey sang their sean-nós songs. It was changed times in comparsion to 1802 when Patrick Lynch went across bog and moor with pockets full of tobacco and whiskey in order to coax songs from the local people. But more of that later.

Erris is a veritable treasure house of folklore. The legends and tales of the past and many old songs still flourish. From early days the Irish Folklore Commission (founded in 1935) under the guidance of the late Séamus Ó Duilearga collected stories of sea and shore from men like John Henry of Kilgalligan.[1] Séamus Ó Catháin was instrumental in getting the help of dedicated men such as Tomás a Burc of Portacloy,

Michael Ó Seighin of Ceathru Thaidhg, Mártán Ó Conghaile of Kilgalligan, Micheál Ó Corrdhuibh and his sons Leon and Annraoi, Padraig Ó Luinigh, Liam Mac Coisdeala, Proinnsias de Burca and Ciarán Bairéad.

John Henry was a native of Dún Caocháin, an isolated part of the barony of Erris.[2] The earliest settlement there dates back to 3000 B.C. When the history of the area grips you, there is no turning back but there is an ache to learn more and to wish that the people of Ireland would view north west Mayo as one of the greatest sources of our heritage.

The arrival of Cromwell in Ireland 1647 had a dreadful effect all over Ireland but especially in the Erris peninsula. The Barrett family lost their lands to James Shaen, whose descendants married into the Bingham family. Sir Richard Bingham of 16th century infamy was two hundred years dead and tales of his terrible deeds lived on in the folklore when Major Bingham came to the Mullet. His yoemen were extremely unpopular in the Mullet in 1796.[3] They preyed on local people and no woman was safe. The Major built Bingham Castle at Elly. When he first came to Bangor he gave three plots for the building of a town there. He built a home there known as Bangor Lodge. There was little done to improve the lot of the tenants. But the landlords of the Mullet set their minds to opening up access to markets.

The only roads were the "Bealaigh Garbha" which met at Bangor and in winter were well nigh impassable. One entrance into Erris was from the South through Ballycroy, where the traveller had to cross the ferry into Tullaghaun. The most ancient way into Erris was from Newport. It was intersected by about twenty rivers. In 1817 Bingham set about building a road from Castlebar to the Mullet. There was another "Bealach Garbh " along the Owenmore, connecting Bangor with Tyrawley.[4] There were no roads west of Castlebar and therefore no markets. In 1820 the bridge at Bellacorick (known as the "Musical Bridge") was completed. Then the Major built a town and called it Binghamstown but it went into decay before it was completed. In 1820 he was granted a patent to hold a fair every month.[5] He decided to charge a toll on all those using it. This gave Binghamstown a new name, An Geata Mór which is its name in Irish to this day. In spite of these efforts the fortunes of the Binghams declined.

This was the situation in north-west Mayo when Patrick Lynch was employed by the committee of the Belfast Harp Festival to visit Connacht in search of the words of Irish songs. Many of those on that committee were United Irishmen, Wolfe Tone, William Drennan, Samuel MacTier, John and Henry Sheares, Edward Fitzgerald, Henry Joy McCracken and Thomas Russell (known as The Man from God Knows Where). The United Irishmen were mostly Presbyterian and had little use for the Dublin Anglo-Irish

Government. Another prominent organiser was Dr. James McDonnell. The festival took place in the Assembly Rooms in Belfast in 1792.[6] Ten harpers came together to play.

Edward Bunting was employed by the committee of the Harp Society to note down the music. He was to follow Lynch, who was proficient in Irish, into Connacht and take down the music of the tunes. He intended to publish a collection of airs and melodies after his return from the west. His chief backer in this enterprise was Thomas Russell who appeared to have an overall view of Ireland incorporating her culture into every-day life. Even when he was in Newgate prison, Russell maintained an interest in Bunting's work.

Lynch stayed the first night of his journey with Bunting's brother Anthony, in Drogheda. Here he got directions and introductions. The route he was directed to take was from Drogheda to Cullen, Kingscourt, Cavan, Swanlinbar, Manorhamilton, Collooney, Ballina, Killala, and around the Co. Mayo to Newport and Castlebar. He left Drogheda on Monday, 26 April, 1802. He stopped at Slane and continued to Navan a distance of fourteen miles. He seems to have had no means of transport as he says he was affected greatly by the rain. He called to Dr. Plunkett, the Catholic Bishop of Meath but he was not there. On Tuesday, from Navan he journeyed to Kells and Virginia, eighteen miles. On Wednesday he went by Cavan to Belturbet, twenty-one miles. On Thursday he went to Black Lion, twenty miles. On Friday, to Manorhamilton which he estimated as eighty-two miles from Drogheda. On Friday evening he travelled six miles to Killargy to meet a very old man called Billy Bartley who had been at Carolan's death bed back in 1738. He had a letter of introduction from Mr. Pat O Connor for Bartley from whom he got six songs described by Lynch as "some of the best of Carolan's". Lynch stayed in the local public house, where he got a further sixteen songs, until the following Monday.[7]

Lynch continued his journey through Dromahaire and Collooney to Screen in Sligo where he got five songs from a farmer called James Dowd. That night he dispensed some whiskey and he got eggs and good potatoes and a bed in the barn. He stopped at a public house eight miles from Ballina. He had a letter of introduction from Miss Bellew to her brother the Right Rev, Dr. Bellew, Ballina. He dined with him and his clergy. He was advised to travel to Erris across the county and to the Mullet, the most westerly part of Mayo. And so he made his way to Erris, 'áit iargualta', a wild, wind-swept, mountainous, country with the 'white horses' of the Atlantic lashing against the rocks. Some of the people of that area were suspicious of him. He had difficulties at a post office where a letter should have reached him. The Bishop of Killala had recom-mended him. The owner of the Post Office was a sergeant and he may have thought Lynch was a United Irishman in disguise. It was all sorted out, but it shows the diffi-culties of being unknown and travelling in strange area in 1802. He travelled from

Crossmolina towards Erris. Dulaig was his next stop where there was only one house where he stayed and gave the owner some whiskey and tobacco. He travelled four miles the next day crossing a great moor the likes of which he never saw before. He was exhausted as he crossed the Owenmore River and as he found himself getting weaker he saw a very poor cabin on the side of a mountain. Here he rested for awhile and gave some tobacco for one song. He bought a half-pound of tobacco for one and seven pence.[8]

When Lynch got as far as Daniel Kelly's near the entrance of the Mullet he was given food food fit for a king- potatoes, eggs and fresh oysters with plenty of milk and butter. His comment was "they made no use of bread in this country". By June 3rd Lynch had collected forty-seven songs. He came to the Mullet to Richard Barrett of Corn, beside An Geata Mór, or Binghamstown. After waiting some days there he got six great songs from him. There were a great many men of property in the Mullet, but he was not invited to any gentlemens' houses, as it was not their custom to invite anyone below their rank. Barrett was a good singer, a born poet and equal to any bard in the country and in Lynch's opinion he had more songs than any man in Connacht.

Coming to the Abhann Mór (Owenmore) the flood was too high to cross so he stayed in the house of Patrick Deane for the night by the riverside. Deane sent his horse with Lynch over the river the next day. He crossed the Craggy Mountain and the roughest road ever travelled. He saw no house for sixteen miles but one poor cabin in the distance. Having waded to the knees through or across seven rivers he arrived at Strathfern but he could not find any place to stay. He crossed a watery marsh to find one old woman with about a dozen kids. Here he got a good drink of milk and continued to trudge the road for another four miles to Newport.

At Newport Lynch had some difficulty at the post office. The people believed he was really on a political mission from the McCracken family and the Belfast United Irishmen. Lynch wrote to McCracken and Bunting as his means was running out. He needed money to survive otherwise he might not get the songs he needed. This he emphasised again and again.

Because he had not heard from Belfast, Lynch wrote to Mary McCracken, sister of Henry Joy McCracken and to Dr. James McDonnell stating what work he had completed. Reaching Castlebar he made good progress and stayed there ten days and got nearly fifty songs. In all he had acquired one hundred and one songs by this time including six from blind Redmond Staunton, one of which was a proper copy of 'Tigherna Muigho', two from Pat Gibbons, two from John Moran, and one from the father of his landlord Mr. M'Myler. On Wednesday June 9th he bought a half-pound of tobacco, and made an excursion eight miles south of Westport to a mountainous place called Drummin. In John Gaven's house he got eight songs from Norah Denny, Nancy McLoughlin and Mrs Gaven.

In Coill Mór he got another song from Pat M'Donald. By this time his money had gone to all but a few shillings. In despair he wrote to Mary McCracken in Belfast. He told her that on the 22 June he went to Louisborough and stayed at a public house. The next day he went three miles west looking for a schoolmaster. He got three songs from him. Next day he returned to Louisborough and heard of a blind piper. He met him at Hugh O'Donnell's and took down six good songs from him. He writes that he never found any one who had so great a variety of good old songs and tunes. He said this man would be more useful to Bunting than any man in Connacht. However he was running into debt and he said in the letter:

"My dear Miss Mary, I hope you will see me relieved out of this hobble; and direct to the Rev.Dr. Lynagh, Westport, and it will ever oblige,
    Your humble servant,
    Patrick Lynch

At the same time he wrote to Dr.MacDonnell, Linen Hall Street, Belfast, and asked him to call on John McCracken, as he had not answered his letters of June the 4th and 21st. He had written a letter, and enclosed one hundred and fifty songs with the names of the persons from whom he got them and the places. He wrote a second letter to Mary Cracken. He named some of the songs he had collected from a Mrs Fitzgerald including *The Red Salmon of Loch Erne*.

At last Bunting arrived on 3 July and paid Lynch's bills. They both left Westport, stopped at Partry and then went on to Headford. It would seem that Bunting was driving a light vehicle of some sort. Lynch, it can be assumed had no longer to trudge on foot except occasionally, after the arrival of Bunting. They got seventeen songs from "Blind Billy" which cost six and sixpence. This sum went towards refreshments! They stayed nearly a fortnight in Westport and the time was spent revisiting or interviewing those whose songs had already been taken down. Then they left Westport, and stopped at Partry. They dined together at an inn in Ballinrobe.

Bunting's first collection was published in 1796 and consisted of melodies without words. Lynch got little credit from Bunting for his collections and hardships. But it must be noted that Bunting did recognise that the English translations did not represent the spirit of the original Gaelic.[9] Lynch went back to Belfast where he taught Russell Irish. He later moved to Loughlinisland where he lived with his children.

There was a classical school in the Loughlinisland area run by The O'Loingsigh (Lynch) family before the end of the eighteenth century. Latin and Irish were the principal subjects. It was here that the Bishop of Down and Connor Dr. Padraig Mac Mailáin was educated. He was born in the parish of Loughlinisland in 1752. Mgr James O Lavery gives an account of him in his book Historical Account of Down and Connor. Successive members of the Lynch family had kept this famous classical school. According to the tradition of the area, the ruins of the Lynch house are on the lands of O'Toole family. Eamon O Toole, who lives in the parish of Loughlinisland, says his grandfather Edward was brought up by the Lynch family.[10]

About 1794 Patrick Lynch was teaching in the Belfast Academy and privately in several families.Thomas Russell introduced him to the scholar Whitley Stokes and they both worked on the translation of the Gospel of Saint Luke and many other religious books. When published Stokes never gave any credit to Lynch. In 1803 Russell was arrested. At his trial Lynch said that he knew him and that he was sorry to see him in the dock. Russell was hanged in Downpatrick on 21 October 1803. In 1806 Lynch settled in Dublin and started a private school. He became secretary to the newly founded Gaelic Society and among the members were Fr. Paul O'Brien, who was the great grand nephew of Carolan, Edward O'Reilly, Theophilus Ó'Flanagan and Fr. Denis Taffe. A hundred years later the Gaelic League compilers of phrase books drew on the joint grammar of Lynch and Neilson. It contains a fine Madden version of the famous poem "Deirdre's Lament". Dr. R.R. Madden, historian, in United Irishmen Vol II said "Patrick Lynch was apprehended and fixed upon to identify Russell, in which transaction Lynch was entirely blameless in my opinion." It has been said that Lynch gave evidence very reluctantly. Perhaps further research on Patrick Lynch would cast him in a different light. In 1808 he had employment as a copyist of Gaelic mss in Trinity College and in 1810 he was doing the same in the Royal Irish Academy. He died in 1829.

The West Mayo Poets
Richard Barrett (Riocard Bairéad)
Barrett's name is famous in Mayo. Apart from having a wealth of old songs he composed many of his own. He was married twice, and had children by both wives. His first wife was Anne Tollet, mentioned in his poem *Oiche an t-Sneachta Mhóir agus na Gaoithe Móire*. Barrett was a United Irishman and he was jailed for three months in Castlebar. According to James Kearney writing in the Gaelic Journal 1894, Barrett was a native of Leam, seven miles from Belmullet. The parish priest of Killala the very Rev, Patrick A. O'Reilly had for many years gathered much information about Richard Barrett which would have been lost but for him. T.F. O'Rahilly put together what he had to say with accounts from Mr.Timony and Mr. Kearney in The Gaelic Journal 1894, as well as material from oral tradition. He got this information from a pupil of Barretts – John O'Toole and from a very old woman who lived to be the age of 104. The old lady said Barrett was a pleasant person.

Barrett died on 8 December 1819 and was buried at Holy Cross cemetery a few miles outside Bellmullet. About fifteen years ago the people of Erris started an "Éigse Riocárd Bairéad". On the weekend of August 19, 1983 the plaque on the grave of Riocárd Bairéad was unveiled by Siobhán Mc Kenna. It was an unforgettable day.

Preab san Ól was a popular drinking song of Richard Barrett.[11] He made this song for Fr. Ned Deane the parish priest of Bealdura and for Minister Maxwell of the same parish.

Is iomaí slí sin a bhíos ag daoine,
Ag cruinniú píosaí is ag déanamh stóir,
is a luighead a smaoinígheas ar ghiorra an tsaoghail seo
Is go mbéidh siad sínte faoi leac go fóill.

Má's tighearna tíre, diúic nó rí thú,
Ní cuirfidhear pinginn leat is tú 'dul faoin bhfód.
Mar sin 's dá bhrí sin níl beart níos críonna
ná bheith go síorruidhe 'cur preab san ól.

Preab san Ól

His theme is that people gather wealth in many ways and seldom think that they cannot take any of it to the grave. So forget about wealth and drink to your heart's content!

John Bernard Trotter in his account of his journeys[12] through Mayo two hundred years ago says that he met Barrett whom he describes as "a venerable poet of Erris" who wrote in Irish and English. Barrett according to Trotter lived with his books as companions and was quite content on five acres of land. Incidentally Trotter founded and subsidised The Dublin Harp Society.

Tarraingt na Mónadh

This poem arose out of the following circumstances. Major Bingham the Erris landlord encountered Barrett when the latter was preparing the ground for the taking home of the turf. When Bingham saw what he was doing he said with bitterness and anger "It's not with songs you'll turf that, Barrett".

Barrett spread the word and the neighbours gathered in "meitheal from Fál Mór to Gleann na Muaidhne" and each one's turf was home and in ricks by midday the next day. After this incident Riocárd Bairéad composed the song.

Tarraingt na mónadh

Tá mo chuid mónadh gróigthe ar na portaigh
'Na shomadáin comh-chruinn 's gan fód ar bith fliuch dhí
Tá mo chroídhe brónach ó mhór- obair thuirseach,
Ag réabadh na mbóithrí d'á ndóghadh 's d'á losgadh.

Tabhair sgéal go Bárr-Thrághadh chuig mo cháirdí Síol gConaill
Chun Stiophán 's chun Dáithí, an dá Phádraic 's a mbunadh,
Go bhfuil mé go mo chrádh' a's gach lá a' dul 'un donacht.
'S mara gcuiridh orm tártháil, tá 'n cás go ro-dhona.

Athruigh do chursa 'gus stiúr go Muigh Reathain
'Gus innis go múinte 's go ciúin go Jack Tallot
Chomh maith 's dá mba rún é 's nár chliú é le n-aithris
Go dtáinic an Púca 's gur mhúin sé ar an mbearraic

Téirigh chuig Seán ó Raghallaigh, fear dílís is cneasta,
'S ná dearmad a chaomhthach (sic)'s tabhair na mílte céad beannacht;
Dá mbéadh fhios aige an chaoi bhfuil na daoine 'ghá lagadh
Do chuirfeadh sé aníos chugam trí fichead capall.

"Éirigh, a Mhartain, agus réidtigh ar an gcapall,
Go dtéigh tú Dia Céadaoin léithe 'un an Bhearraic;
Má's fíor maise, an sgéal úd, is sgéal é nach maith dhúinn,
A's má imthigeann Dick Bairéad, cé dheanfas do theagasc?

Téigigh chuigh Hanraoi anonn go Belmullet
A's casfar leat Aindí, 's annsacht gach duine é;
Má ghnídh sé shake hands leat bí thankful and civil
Acht má théigheann sé 'un stainne' leat: God Damn the black devil !

Ta mo chruach déanta ar éadan an bhealaigh
Tá cúig coiscéim déag agus céad troigh ar fad inntí;
Chuirfí tnúth ar an Major dá mhéad a chuid feara;
'Sé mheasaim go mbéidh sé níos réidheachta faoin Deachmhaidh.

Cúig capall déag agus céad do bhí ag tarraingt.
Bhí fir I n-a léinteachaibh gléigeala ag freastal;
Bhí tuilleadh 's dáréag ann ag réidhteach 's ag crapadh;
'S béidh cuimhne go h-éag ar Dhiardaoin na gCapall!

Eoghan Cóir is a satire about an agent of the Binghams. He was more than heavy-handed on the tenants and throughout the area was always a nasty, cruel man. Even though Eoghan Cóir had died fifty years before Bairéad was born he was remembered as being greedy, badmouthed and liked to see people cornered. If you did not know the story you would think he was man's best friend.

Eoghan Cóir

Nach é seo an scéal deacrach sa tír seo,
Le anacair , croí agus brón
Ó fhágas tú Crocán an Líona
Go dtéigh tú go dtí an Fál Mór.
A leithéid de sgreadaoil is de chaoineadh
Ní chualas ariamh go fóill
Ó cailleadh ár gcara sa tír seo,
An duine bocht maol Eoghan Cóir

About the year 1800 there was a great heavy fall of snow accompanied by high winds which had never been seen before in living memory.

Oidhche an t-sneachta mhóir agus na gaoithe móire [13]

Dá mbeitheá-sa agam in aimsir na gaoithe,
Is ann a bhí an caoineadh bocht a's an gleó,
Ag Nansaí Tallot 's í a'gearradh na gaoithe
Nuair nach raibh tuighe aicí le h-aghaidh a chuid bó.
Ar dhearcadh dhí síos ar an mBuidhe 's ar an Deirg,
D'árduigheadh uirri daormhach ba gaolmhar le mire,
Bhí Dickey bocht sínte faoi dhídean na pluide,
'S thug sí de'n teanga sin robadh no dhó.

Dubhairt Seán Dubh Ó h-Ógáin go raibh aige ortha
Chuirfeadh 'n ghaoth mhór a's an sneachta ar gcúl,
Nuair a chuaidh sé ar a ghlúinibh d'árduigh an cuaifeach
Gur stad do'n devotion go léigeadh sé faoi.
Dá gcluintheá an sníomhadh a bhíodh ag na creatacha',
Le fóirneacht na gaoithe 's go snaidhmeadh gach creat aca;
'S é dubhairt len a chaoimtheach: "Ó's daoine gan teach sinn
árdaigh leat Naidí a's teanam 'un siubhal ".

Cé thiocfadh 'steach acht Antóin ó Gaibhtheacháin
's chonnaic sé Seán bocht faoi dhuibhshion's faoi smúid
D'fiafruigh sé 'r fuaduigheadh a theach no a cheardcha,
Nó a' dtainic an áirnéis abhaile o'n dúmhaigh.
"Níor tháinic, a bhráthair Mhic Adhaimh agus Mharcuise,
Plúr Muintir Gáibhtheachain a's árd-scaith na' gEachmharcach,
Seo sé pingine bhán dhuit,'s tabhair Dárbí ó'n t-sneachta chugam,
'S déanfa mé thairis sin stopple a's lúb"

Sean, the blacksmith in Binghamstown, was a hardworking man and good at his trade. It was said that he rarely did anything without pay. One day Barrett visited the forge and he asked Seán to make a half dozen pig rings for him. This he did. When he was offered him money he refused to accept it. Barrett was very impressed, so, he thought it would only be right to 'make' a song for him.[14]

An Gabha

Is agam-sa atá 'n chomharsa
Is córa 'gus is ceirte d'a bhfuil sa ' tír;
Duine measamhail cneasta módhamhail,
Is cródha i neart agus I ngíomh.
Ní eachrannach agus ní gleódhach
I n-am póite nó óil é,
Lá an mhargaidh, I dtigh an ósta
No Domhnach an Lógh';
Acht le carthannas agus síor-chórtas
Ag scapadh airgid agus 'óir orainn
Chleacht tú sin, 's go raibh go deo agat,
A leoghan, Seán Gabha!

Ní fhacthas Seán ariamh as órdú
Ná ar nós ar bhféidir magadh dhéanamd faoi;
'N-a scraiste ar thaobh an bhóthair
Ní raibh a thón ariamh in abar nó indígh,
I n-aimsir fearthann, sneachta, nó ghaoth mhór
Tiocfaigh Jack abhaile go laghach cródha,
Níor fhág ariamh a hata amuigh
A mhaide, wig nó a bhróga,
'S ní bheadh ceo ar Sheán Gabha
gnídh sé an briogún, an bior mónadh
An bior rosta, agus fearsad túirne lín.

'S É Fáth Mo Bhuartha [15]

Is é fáth mo bhuartha nach bhfaighim cead cuairte ort
Sa ghleanntán uaighneach mar a mbíonn mo ghrá
Bíonn mil ar luachair ann, im ar uachtar,
go tús an Fhómhair bíonn na crainn fé bhláth.
Níl gaoth aduaidh ann, níl sneachta crua ann,
Tá caladh is cuan ann ag long is ag bád.
Mar thuilleadh bua ann níl turas cruaiche ann
Ag an té a dhéanfadh suas le mo mhuirnín bán.

Is é dúirt mo stór liom ó bhí tú óg deas
Go ndéanfá foghlaim ar éalú liom.
Is nach mbíonn tráthnóna nó maidin fhómhair
Nach tú an réalt eolais a bhíos 'dul romham.
Ag siúl na mbánta is na gcoillte cnómhar
Ní bheadh orm brón nó duibheagán croí
Ach mé bheith pósta ar mo mhíle stóirín.
Is mo lámh go bródúil ar a brollach mín.

There is an older song than this one, the words of which I got from Michéal Ó Seighin in Ceathrú Thaidg. Is agallamh beirte é idir Dick Bairead ag moladh na Léime and Bríd Ní Dhómhnaill ag moladh na Corrshléibhe. It is also to be found in the writings of Padráig Breathnach collected by Micheál Ó Tiománaidhe in *Ámhráin an Íarthair* in the middle of the nineteenth century. Padraig was born and reared on Inis Gheith. He was a seanchaí and a good singer.

Adúirt Dick Bairéad: -

> *'Se fáth mo bhuartha nach bhfaighim cead cuairt'*
> *Ins an ngleann atá an-uaignech ina mbíonn mo ghrá*
> *A bhfuil mil ar luachair' im ar uachtar,*
> *I dtus an fhuaicht bhíonn na ba dhá ndáir.*
> *Nach deas an chaoi bheith i measc na maolchnoc;*
> *Is na ba dhá ndídean ar fud na maigh:*
> *Mar seo a bhíonn sé an tortan cíbe,*
> *Tá an coileach fraoigh ann, a chearc is a h-ál.*

Adúirt Bríd Ní Dhomhnaill: -

> *Is deas an siamsa bheith ag amharc ar flít;*
> *Cidh gurb olc an críoch theanns ortha i dtráth. :*
> *Nuair thigeas dibirt as neart na gaoithe*
> *Is bíonn na daoine á gcur amach sa tsnamh .*
> *Níl druinn ar uair ann, níl sneachta aduaidh ann,*
> *Tá caladh is cuan ann ag loing is ag baid:*
> *Tá tuilleadh buaidhe ann, níl turas cruaiche ann,*
> *An té dhéanfadh suas len a chailin bán.*
>
> *Adúirt Dick Bairéad:-*
> *Ní ar shliabh ná ar fhíorchloch a bhíonns mo mhian-sa,*
> *Acht ar thalta aoibhne a mbíonn gach meas ag fás;*
> *Tá an chuach ag blaoch ann ar bharraí craoibh an*
> *Tá cruithneacht mhaol ann is coirce bán,*
> *Tá an fia is an lao ann, tá na bric ina scaoth ann,*
> *,Tá an eala is aoibhne ar an loch is í ag snamh,*
> *Tá bheach go críonna ann is a h-árus déanta,*
> *Is mil da taomadh ann go moch gach lá.*

Arsa Bríd:-

> *Is álainn Corrshliabh i dtús an gheimhridh,*
> *Ní bhíonn leac oighir air ná sneachta aduaidh,*
> *Is ceolmhar traona ann, an chuach is an londubh,*

Faoi bharraí crainn ann ins an duilliúr rua.
Is binn guth gadhair ann ag tóraiocht eilite,
Is an fia ins an áit sin ag rith chun siúil,
Is ann a thionnscaionns gach sruth glan aibhne,
An bradán bruinngheal is an breac ar lúth.

Dún Dónaill was collected by Peadar Bairéad in Belmullet; It is about Dún Dónaill in Erris.[16]

Dún Dónaill

Án t-ochtú lá dh'earrach bhí an bas ag tíocht liom,
Teann mé leis an gCarnach go liginn ann mo scíth,
Dhá mbeinnse thiar thar Ghearradh nó láimh le Liam Ó Caramgnaigh,
Is mé a bheadh lúfar aigeantach ó d'fágfainnse teach Néill.
D'ólfainn sláinte Chaitlín le gradam faoin a comhar,
'Sé mo léan gan mé i nGleann Chaisil óir is ann a bhéinn go macrasach,
Ceol, sport, is aiteas ann le fáil ó Shéamas Óg.

Níor fhás sé aníos as cré, adhmad, péine ná mahogany
Nach bhfuighfi ar an Screadaidh is crann le cur ar loing,
Gur dh'aoibhneas an tsaoil uile fo léir a bheith in aice leis,
Ceolta na meachan ag déanamh áras ins gach tom.
A Dhia is a Mhuire, ná bhfuil sé i gCuige Chonnacht
Áit ar bith is deise ná é anall ón Oileain Úr,
Go dtige athrú ar an bplainéid is sláinte a bheith in aice leis,
Is boladh ó na húlla ins an dún ar bhoilg lae.

Nuair a bhí mé in mo tide water le Ceithearnaigh go hAlbain,
Ag imeacht chun gach station is mo season running good,
An trua libh mé a bheith i ngéibhinn nó ná léigí amach sa bhfairraige,
Ó thigeach orainn gairfean go n-athraíodh aríst.
Casadh dhomsa Brógán at chóstaí Meiriocá,
As Iorras thú , a stócaigh, nó an bhfuil eolas agat ann?
Is fada mé ar mo thuairisc ins gach baile cuain dhá ndeachaigh tú,
I caithfimid an fomhar seo i nDún Dónaill le greann.

Barrett remembers, as he is is dying, all the places he has been in and all those he met, and he longs for Dún Dónaill, for the scent of the flowers, the call of the cuckoo, the beauty of Néifinn and it's his desire to spend the autumn there.

Oídhche Sheagháin Uí de Dhiarmuda concerns a great storm one night in Carn. Séan Mac Diarmada was working for Barrett. Barrett praises him in this song for going under the bed instead of helping Barrett and his wife to save the house!

Oidhche Sheagháin Uí de Dhiarmuda [17]

Dhá bhfeictheá Dick máigistir ar a mhasa is ar a liarca,
Le pianta in a chnámha 's gan tracht ar na fiacla,
'Sé dúirt Nancy a bhean is maith mar a thárlaidh ,
Tá an tadh orainne i mbliadhna tá 'cuile shórt tárrthuigh ag Seaghán Ó De
Dhiarmada.

D'éirigh Máire Ní Phaidín i lár an mheadhon oidhche
D'amharc sí ar an ngarrdha's ní bhfuair sí ann ach iarmhar.
"Cuirim- se scread chráidhte ar ádhmad's ar iarann,
Is trua géar gan mo Sheághan-sa mar Sheaghán Ó De Dhiarmada.

D'éirigh Micheál Mharthain I lár an mheadhoin oidhche'
I leabhaidh "neamna páirte" is é thracht ar an rí-dhiabhal,
Mart is marbh fhaisg ort a sglabhuidhe mí-rialta,
'S mo léan gab fear in d'ait agam mar Sheaghán Ó De Dhiarmada.

Séamus and Dominic Cosgair

The brothers Dominic and Séamus Cosgair were poets. They were highly educated although they never went to school. They learned Latin, French, and German as well as English and Irish, by the fireside. Séamus was shopkeeper in An Geata Mór and played music on the violin and bagpipes and was also a dancer. Dominic was a farmer and excelled at bullet throwing and high jumping. His best song is *Scéimh Rinn na Feirste*. Seamus composed the poem *An Abhainn Mhór* which was collected by the folklorist Seamus Ó Duilearga in Chicago in 1939. Ó Duilearga had gone to the States hoping to meet Micheál Ó Gallchobhair (1860-1938) who was originally from Coill Salach in Erris and who was known to have a number of Barrett's poems. Unfortunately by the time Seamus arrived Micheál had died. However he was brought to meet Micheál's three sisters one of whom , Máire, sang *An Abhainn Mhór*. He recorded it and other material on the edifon.[18]

An Abhainn Mhór

Céad slán leat, a Abhainn Mhór,
Is é mo bhrón gan mé anocht le do thaobh!
Nach iomaidh sin bóithrín caol uaigneach
A gabhail eidir mé is í.
Nach ann a bheadh an spórt Dia Domhnaigh,
Is go mall tidheacht na hoidhche,
Bheadh gloineadh os cionn bhuird ann,
Is comhluadar geanamhail le suidhe

Tá mo rúitíní gearrtha is ní áirighim,
Tá m'ioscada fann.
Ó shíor-árdughadh an mhála
Leis an bpian atá 'mo dhroim,
Tá mé I bhfad ó mo cháirde,
Is níl áit agam a leigfinn mo scíth,
Is níl ball ar bith slán díom nach bhfuil fágtha,
Nó fuagradh a bheith tinn.

Bhéarfadh mé mi mhóide is dócha liom
Nach mbrisfidh mé choidhche,
I gcomhluadar ban óg go deo,
Ní shuidfidh mé síos,
Is mé cráidheadh leo I dtus m'óige,
Mo chreach, fairíor,
Is gurbh iad cailíní Bhun an Bhóthair.
Mhúin an t-eolas dom amach goTráighlí.

Tá mo chóta mór stróichte ó Dhomhnach,
Go talamh liom síos,
Is an té chuirfeadh cóir air 'sé mo bhrón
Tá sé i bhfad as mo lín,
Níl aon fhear a phósadh mo stór,
Is mé bheith ina dhiaidh
Nach mbainfinn an tsrón de,
Nó ba mhór mhór a cháirde sa tír.

Nuair theidheanns an t-aos óg
'S mo bhrón, amach ins an lá
Méadaíonn ar mo dhólas,
Is réabthar ar mo mhíle stór
Nuair smuainighim ar mo mhíle, stór,
Bhéarfadh ól dom is imirt ar chlár,
Go bhfuil sí ar fear eile pósta,
Is gur treoruidhe bocht mise atá le fán.[19]

Padraic Daeid
Padraic was born three miles from Belmullet.[20] *Nóra Dheas na gCraobh Fholt Úi Bheaidh* is his best known poem. He was living on Inis Bigil with his mother. He went from there to Ulster where he learned the trade of tailoring. When he returned he was wearing a blue suit. After that he was known as the Blue Tailor. He spent his time going from house to house in Achill tailoring and composing songs. He died at eighty and is buried in Uachta Acla. He composed this song for Nora ní Bhéaidh who was living in Acaill. It was said she gave him his first meal and he on the road travelling early in the morning.

Nora dheas na gCraobhfholt ní Bhéaidh

Nora dheas na gCraobhfholt ní Bhéaidh
Bhí mé lá breá gréine,
Is mé a'triall ag dul chun aonaigh,
Is casadh liom an réalt gan smál.
D'fhiosraigh mé den spéirbhean,
An í bainríon óg ón nGréige í
An í Juno,Pallas, Nó Venus í nó an gheall?

Tá a grua ar dhath na gcaor,
Is a leaca a bhí dhá réir,
Mar atá an eala is í ag éirí den snamh.
Is dúirt sí liom go céillí,
"níl neach ar bith den mhéid sin,
Ach Nóra dheas na gCraobhfholt ní Bhéaidh".

Sheinnfeadh sí ar théadraí,
Le meabhair chinn is méara
Fidil, fliút ar aon staid amháin.
Is riarfadh sí na céadta
Gan gruaim a chur ina héadan,
Nóra Dheas na gCraobhfholt Ní Bhéaidh'

Micheál MacSuibhne

MacSuibhne was born on Omey Island; Iomaidh Feicín in Irish. This island has connections with other areas, the first being Leyney in the Diocese of Achonry Co.Sligo.
St. Feicin patron of Fore in Meath founded a monastery in Omey in the seventh century, (Colgan's Acta SS 135.)

He was the founder of several small abbeys, one in Easdara in Sligo and one in Cong.
From Hardiman's notes we find that between Inistuirk and Omey islands an arm of the
sea runs to the castle of Down where there is a harbour for shipping. The church of
Athdearg near the castle was in ancient times the parish church, but now the parish
church is at Omey. MacSuibhne was a contemporary of Barrett. Much of the informa-
tion on his work comes from the Galway scholar, James Hardiman.[21] Master Slopers
Whiskey, Abhrán an Phúca, Bainis Pheigi Ní h-Eaghra and Máirín Seoighe are
MacSuibhne's best known poems. Here is one verse of *Máirín Seoighe*.

> A gabháil trí Chonga do dhearc mé an chúilfhionn
> Ba mhian na cúige léi síos go drúcht.
> Bhí a fholt a' casadh léi síos
> Agus blas a' tsiúcra bhí ar a póig.

Fuisce Mhaistir Sloper[22]

Ar meisce dom, 's níor mhiste liom,
Gach lá saoire, is Domhnach;
Ag éirí suas ar maidin
Is ag luí síos tráthnóna;
Is é bheir croí is misneach dúinn,
Thógas cíos is tinneas dínn, Is ní ólfainn deor den uisce,
Dá bhfaighinn fuisce Mháistir Sloper.

Níor fhás aon phór trí thalamh riamh
Chomh maith leis an ngráinne eorna
Dá fheabhas an bia le hithe é
Is fearr an deoch le h-ol é
Bhuail sé Tuaim is Sacsana
Is a bhfuil as sin go hAlbain
Rún mo chroí is m'anam é
Cuid fuisce Mhaistir Sloper.

Abhrán an Phúca

Eireóchaidh mé air maidin a n-ainm an domhnaigh
Agus rachfaidh mé a chomhnaidhe air chnocáinín bhan,
Déanfaide mé teach ann ar leathtaobh an bhóthair,
A bhfogus do'n chomhgar a bhus agus thall.
A n-áit a mbeidh agam fear bhealaigh agus bhóthair,
Caidreamh lucht eolais fear loinge agus báid,
Biaidh sgol ag lucht ealadhan 's ag ógánaígh óga
A lorg an eolais ag teacht air mo shráid.

Is é iomrádh na g-cailleach is na seandaoine críonna,
D'fhág mearbhall air m'intinn, is néull ann mo cheann,
Tá a rádh go bhfuil an Púca ann ó aimsir na díleann,
Go Bhfacaidh na daoine é, acht ní fhuil fhios cia an t-am;
Níor bh-é sin dob ait liom-sa a teacht ráithe an gheimhre,
A bheith déanamh íosbairt a stigh an mo shráid.

Chuaidh an Púca go Gaillimh air maidin Dia haoíne,
Ag iarraidh adhbhar bríste de'n éadach dob fheárr,
Thainig an deireanas, is thuit air an oíghche,
Agus thosaigh sé agcaoíne n-uair a d'imhtigh an lá;
Bhí sé ag sgreadadh 's ag imtheach thar timchiol,
Go bh-fághadhsé dídean astigh leis na mnaibh,
Seóladh go hÉachrúis is go baile Conrai é,
Amach tré chnoc Mhaoínis is thort Innis Meadhon.

The wedding of Peggy O'Hara is an amusing composition in which MacSuibhne describes the preparations for the feast - a rich assortment of dresses for the bride, an abundant supply of wine and whiskey, beer in boatloads, tea and spices of all kinds, including 'nutmeg and saltpetre' with all the necessary apparatus of' knives and forks', pipes, tobacco, cards, backgammon boxes and 'bands of music', fish, fowl, all kinds of meat from the ox to the badger. The guests consist of the great Milesian families of Connacht. Hardiman said the spirit of this poem would be entirely lost by translation.

Bainis Pheigi ní h-Eaghra[23]

A Labhrais Fheichín gluais go tapaidh
Ó 's tú tá chum a dhéanta'
Tabhair leat abhaile ádhbhar rascail,
Agus clóca fáda síoda,
Broga 's patens,cnotaidh gallda ,
Agus ribinghe deasa tríotha ,
Gloues is bobs is gach aon nídh deas
Dár shóghann d'aon bhean san righeacht.
Bíodh sin agad pompedóte,
Spangles, silc is dres-cap mór.
Poudered hairpin,uedgepomatum
Muff maith déanta chum a ghléasta
Le h- agaidh fear a chórúghadh'

Sgior de sgiorradh síos go Sligeach
'S tabhair O'Conchubhair tréan leat,
Brianaigh, Dálaigh, Flaithbheartaigh, Mállaigh,
O'Cearbhaill 's O'Néill leat;
Bíodh leat MacCártaigh, Tighearna an Chláir
O'Ruairc aníos ó'n mBréifne,
Sin Ó'hEaghra, MacSuibhne Fánaid.

Is Clann Dhonchadh na Céise
Bíodh Strongbonians leat go leor,
Muintir Cromell, gídh nár cóir
An meid d'á g-cine nach g-cuirim an suime
Dheirim ar fad go léir dhóibh.

Nach mór an dearmad rinne an fear
Do chuaidh ag cruinniúghadh an fhéasta,
Hugo, Maria, Nora ní Fhathartaigh,
Siobhán is maighistreas Daibhis.
Ainndriu, Ruaidhrighe, Brigid ní Bhruadhair, ,
Máire ní Tuathail is Bhenus,
Brigid is Tomás, muintir Lideáin,
Is Steaphán ceann an mhéid sin.
Bíodh gach duine mar chuaidh sé a g-céim,
An-ionad suidhte air leith leis féin,
Gan aon g'á d-taithighe acht filidhe
Flatha is fleasgaidh ealadhna,
Le h-aghaidh aiste a dhéanamh.

In another poem by Michaél Mac Suibhne, he is dissatisfied with himself. He mentions Newfoundland in the poem and perhaps he regretted not going out there.

'Seard deir mo mhuinntir liom do réir a dtuairim
Go dtiúrfad ruaig go Newfoundland.
Níl mé fulannach 'un iompair ualaigh
In obair thuaí ná in gearradh crann.

CHAPTER 9

FROM TEMPO TO MULLACH BÁN

Pléaráca Mhigh Uidhir[1]

D'fhéachainn planda de dhream na righthe.
Bhéarfad cuairt go luath un tíre
Duine le'r b'ionmhuin ceol d'oidhche 's do ló
Cú Chonnacht crodhach, cliúteach, cosantach, pronntach, fáilteach!
Is leis ba mhian ceolta sidhe, lucht óla fíona
A's gach uile dream bheith in aice-sean
Seo a fhreagair cúirteoir sáimh é
A's curadh gan tslás in aimsir ghleó

One of the most important times of Carolan's life was when he visited the Maguires of Tempo in County Fermanagh. The Maguires of Tempo were one of the greatest and most ancient of the Irish clans. Constantine Maguire married the daughter of Everhood Maginnis of Castle William, in Co. Down. He mortgaged the greatest part of his estate to raise a regiment for James 11, but he was killed at Aughrim in 1691. Constantine had a son Brian for whom Carolan composed the following tune.[2]

Brian Maguire

Brian married Bridget Nugent of Coolamber, Co. Westmeath. They had five sons – Brian, Constantine, Robert, Hugh and Philip.   Robert married Elizabeth MacDermot Roe. They had no family.   There is an amazing story from the Tempo Manor estate history archives which I recall here.[3] It concerns Colonel Hugh Maguire son of Brian and Bridget.

He conformed to the Established Church and after serving in the Austrian army he returned to England and in 1745 married a Lady Cathcart. This was her fifth marriage. Hugh was known as the "wicked colonel", because of his treatment of his wife. Far from being satisfied with half of her considerable income, he did his worst to frighten her into handing over a fortune in jewels, and the title deeds of her English property, the Manor of Tewin Water in Hertfordshire. When she refused, he abducted her to Ireland and kept her locked up for some years at Tempo. No one dared interfere. The room where she was kept became an outbuilding.

After his death Lady Cathcart (by then well over seventy) was released, ragged, half starved, and almost deranged, she was able to reveal the details after the death of her husband. Having eventually forced her to tell him that the deeds were in a secret compartment behind the panelling he rushed there and climbed on the table to reach the hidden door. The rusty lock resisted his efforts so he took out a jack knife and forced the panel. The knife slipped and cut his hand. Lockjaw followed. He died in agony. (The great Irish writer Maria Edgeworth based the character of Sir Kit Rackrent on Hugh Maguire.) The Tempo estate eventually passed to his nephew, Philip's son Hugh who was very popular in Fermanagh. But the estate was heavily encumbered by debt to Lady Cathcart's trustees (£11000). The trustees forced the sale of 3,277 acres and also the house.

I and friends visited Tempo in August 1999. What a beautiful place! The drive up the avenue led us past tall leafy trees with glorious undergrowth of shrubs and flowers. The front steps led down to a beautiful lake covered in half circles of water lilies in bloom. The lake itself stretched to meet the wooded area in the distance, as three lovely dogs frolicked in and out of the water. The house is old-world and well kept.

Carolan and the Ulster Poets

It is interesting to note that when Henry Morris was writing of the poets whose works he had heard of, he listed Carolan as one of the Oriel, Breffni and Meath poets. Carolan of course was a Meath man even though he spent many years in Connacht. It is also interesting to know that the counties of Louth, Meath, Armagh, Monaghan and Cavan comprised an Irish speaking district. They had been cut off from other Irish speaking parts in Ireland for three hundred years.[4] The Ulster Plantation had hemmed in this area on the north and northwest, while to the south lay the Pale. Louth and Meath belonged of old to the Pale, but were deeply influenced from their long contact with the Irish all around them. It is wonderful to think of the Irish holding on to their language in the above mentioned counties for so long.

In 1904 at the Dundalk Feis, Mr John Mac Neill complained how little was known of the South Armagh poets going back two hundred years. And it was his opinion that some of these, were men whose poetry was far superior to anything that any poet of his day could produce[5]. Henry Morris mentions fourteen poets of the South Ulster area who are well known today. Seán Ua Neachtain, born in Nobber Co. Meath, 1670-1730, Tadhg Ua Neachtain, son of the last mentioned poet, 1700-1750, Turlough O'Carolan, Nobber, 1670-1738, Niall MacCana,-1700-, The Fews Co. Armagh, Séumas Mac Cuarta -1712-, Farney, Liosmoyle, known as An Dall MacCuarta, Peadar Ua Dóirnín, 1682-1768 who is buried in the ancient Churchyard of Urney near Forkhill, Art Mac Cúmhaigh 1715-1773, of the Fews Co. Armagh, last of the Bards of the O'Neills of Toprass Co. Louth, Pádraic Mac Alindon who died in 1733, a native of the Fews, Fergus Mac Beathadh who wrote the grave-lay for Patrick Mac Alindon, Séamus Mac Ciaran –1750-, Padraigh Ua Prointigh –1732-, An tAthair Pól Ua Briain and Séamas Ua Teibhlin, Kells.[6]

It was Colonel Constantine Maguire of Tempo who arranged that Carolan should visit Co.Louth in order to meet the famous Ulster poets of the eighteenth century and Hardiman tells us how Carolan and Séumas Dall MacCuarta first met. Neither had known each other previously. MacCuarta the composer of *Fáilte don Éan* and *An Londubh Báite* was considered the better poet and Carolan the better musician. After playing for some time on the harps Carolan exclaimed, 'Is binn bog bréagach a rinneas tú' ('your music is soft and sweet, but untrue'). MacCuarta quickly replied 'Is minic a bhíonn an fhírinne féin searbh'- ('even truth itself is sometimes bitter'). The bards soon recognised one another. MacCuarta composed the *Welcome* to Carolan and Padraig Mac Alindon wrote another pleasing poem to commemorate Carolan's visit.[7]

> Dá mhillún fáilte dhaoibh
> O árus Mhéabha, inghean Eochaidh,
> Go fearann Oirghiaill, glúnmhar,
> lé'r b'ionmhuin éuchta Chonc.colui

In a MS. written by Art Bennett was the following poem, which he says is the welcome given by Mac Cuarta.[8]

> Imcian fáilte dhuit mo dháil a ghruaidh corcar nach amhnar
> A ghnis chumhra is áille dreacht, do fíor-fuil uasal Carolan.
> Is mór an scéim thú air leith Chún, go ndeunaid Dia da mairtin
> Aghaidh éigse na h'Eiríne ort,a thuile shléibhe na hintleacht.
> Sruth Shomhna an dá láimh do thogadh lucht easláinte
> Ceatha beaga na meoir maoith, a dhalta uchta na n-aird –righ.
> Go d-tainig an liag loghmhurán do fhíor fhuil uasal Eireamhuin.
> Níl preaban a nealadhun ghrí,nach gcanuidhean sé gan aoinlocht.
> Fáilte dhuit a Thoirealbhaigh, a ghnúis Sóilbhear rleanbhaidh
> A thobair ceoil is fearr slóg, da dtainog air shluaigh Milidh.

It is interesting to note that Art Bennett was a noted craftsman. He built and carved most of the headstones in Creggan graveyard including his own.

Patrick MacAlindon, who is said to have visited Carolan when he was a guest of Mac Cuarta, also wrote an important poem of welcome. Crónán Ó Doibhlin, archivist in the Cardinal Ó Fiaich archives at Armagh Cathedral says this poem is in the "crosántacht" style, a comic or satirical form which is fairly common amongst South East Ulster Poets. The poet wants to

become Ó Cearbhallain's harp.[9] If this were to happen, then, everyone would listen to his sweet tones and he would die a happy man. Then in the last verse he says that if he does not get his wish the consequences for all and for Carolan will be dire! According to tradition Padraig MacAlindon was a farmer and his house was a meeting place for the literary people of the time. His poetry contains much of the style and language of the poetry of the classical poets. (*Moladh Shéamais MacCuarta* is one of his best known works).

Do Thoirdhealbhach Ó'Cearbhalláin and do Bríd Crúis [10]

Mo chreach is mo léan! Ó fheartaibh Dé
Nachar teagaimh mé 'mo dhealbh-chruith;
Ní mar gheall ar shéadaibh acht mar gheall ar mhéaraibh
Dhaltáin éigse Banbha
Nó go nglacfadh sé mé in' ucht go séimh
Ar aiste an Ghaedhil ghloin Cearbhall,
'S do thiocfainn féin dá fhios i gcéin
Mar do rinne an ré-bhean Fearbhlaidhe.

Is maith mo ghleas mar theagmhódh mé
Bheith teist mo scéil a dhearbhú
Ghlachadh spéis díom gach flaith de Gaela
Gan leisce in éirinn armghlan;
Níl Gealt dá Eadroime a chluinfidh m-éacthaí
Nach mbeith seal dá éis go ceannsa,
Le binne as tréithe mo dhaltáin shéimse,
Ach mur ibh má féin deoch dhearmaid.

Ach mura dteagmhóidh an scéal seo ná tallann éigín
Ó mo shearc I gcéin do mo Chealgadh
Danfaidh mé éachtaí agus cluinfear faoi Éirinn
Loscadh, léan agus Marbhadh;
Cluinfear géimneach na gcreach dá ndéanamh
Is beidh sruthanna is sléibhte á ndeargadh
Ó fuil na dtréan mura bhfaighidh mé dom féin
Mo cháfaidh déadghlan dealbhach

Carolan must have been very pleased to be among the Ulster poets. He jokingly said, 'Is leithne ná an spéir mo cháil' meaning 'wider than the heavens is my fame'.He wrote the following poem *Betty MacNeill* when he was on his visit to Co. Louth.

91. Betty MacNeill

Mo chuairt go Baile Í Sgannláin
Is fearrde mé í gcéill 's i dtuigse,
An leanbh dheas na mbacall cas
do árd- fhuil Néill
Is geal a píob 's is caol a mailigh
Betí bhíos le taobh na mara.
Shíolraigh ón aicme sin
Do shár-fhuil Ghaedheal.

Art Mac Cumhaigh (1738-1773), who was bard to the O'Neills of Dunraeva, is the best known of the five Gaelic poets from South East Ulster. He was called "Art na gCeoltai". His poem about Creggan is the National Anthem of South East Ulster. He spent his life as a gardener and as a labourer. His melodious verses were sung with heart moving feeling. National hope was not dead in his day. The people had not become reconciled to English rule as being final. He married his cousin in a Protestant church against the wishes of the parish priest the Rev.Terence Quinn of Creggan. Art wrote the satirical poem "Máire Chaoch" (one eyed Mary) about the priest's sister. He felt he had been badly treated when he went to the priest's house to state his case. Máire was also the priest's housekeeper She was entertaining some 'Buic Mhóra' and Art was taken into the kitchen. This was his reason for writing the satire.

As a result of the satirical poem and the priest's refusal to marry him, Art and his new wife were banished to Howth where they spent some time. Eventually the call of Úr Chill an Chreagáin was too much for them and they returned. Art composed a poem of praise for the priest's sister Mary Quinn and called it "*Cuilfhionn Ní Chúinne*" and this helped to patch up their differences.

Henry Morris gives the background to his great poem *Úir Chill an Chreagáin.* Mac Cúbhaigh was on the run and being hunted by the 'powers that be.' He hid for a night in the O'Neill vault in Creggan graveyard (Urney). So his opening line stating that he slept the previous night in Creggan Churchyard is literally true. The epitaph on his headstone in the churchyard is the last line of the poem: "Gurbh ag Gaeil chúmhra an Chreagáin a leagfar mé i gcré faoi fhód"- "that with the fragrant Gaels of Creggan I will be put in clay under the sod." The music and words of Úir Chill an Chreagáin have an extraordinary beauty. It was a great favourite of the late Cardinal Ó Fiaich.

Ag Úir Chill an Chreagáin 'seadh chodail mé 'raoir faoi bhróin
'S le h-érghidh na maidne thánaic aindhir fa mo dhéin le póg
Bhí gruaidh ghis-dhaithe 'ci, 's laindir 'na ciabh mar ór
B'é aoibhneas an domhain bheith ag amharc air an ríoghan óg.

'A fhial-fhir charthannaigh ná caitear thusa i ndealramh bróin
Ach eirigh go tapaidh is tar liomsa siar 'sa ród;
Go tir-dheas na meala nach bhfuair Gaill cead réim go fóill
Mar bhfaighir aoibhneas ar h-allaoibh do d' mhealladh le siansa cheoil'

'dheas A rioghan mhilis an tú Helen fó 'r treaghdadh slóigh
Nó'n de naoi mna deasa Pharnssuis thú bhí déantai i gclódh
Cá tír 'sa gcruinne ar h-oileadh thú, a reált gan ceó
Le'r mhian leat mo samhuil-se bheith cogarnaidh leat siar 'sa ród?'

Gaels of Creggan

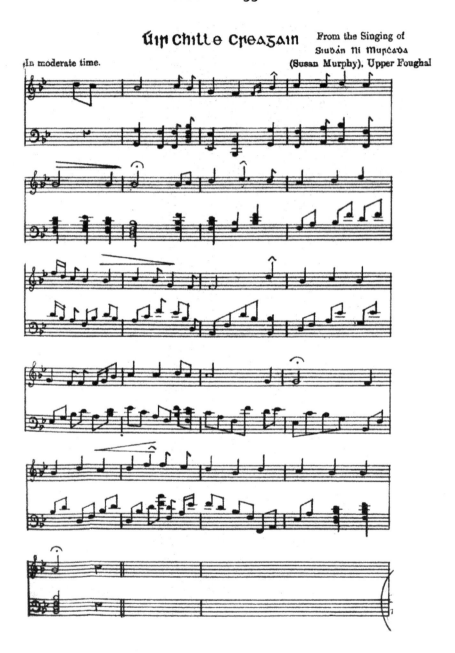

Peadar Ó'Dóirnín (1704-1768) another of the famous South Ulster poets wrote the beautiful love poem *Úrchnoc Chéin Mhic Cáinte* below. Cnoc Chéin Mhic Cáinte is called Killen today. It lies about two miles north of Dundalk.

ÚRCHNOC CHÉIN MHIC CÁINTE

A Phlúir na maighdean is úire gné,
'Fuair clú le scéimh ón Adhamhchlainn
A chúl na bpéarla a rún na héigse
'Dhúblas féile is fáilte;
A ghnúis mar ghréin le dúscadh a' lae
Mhúchas léan le gáire,
'Sé mo chumha gan mé is tú, a shiúr linn féin féin
Sa dún sin Céin Mhic Cáinte.

Táim brúite i bpéin, gan suan, gan néal
De do chumha, a ghéag is áille;
'S gur tú mo roghain i gcúigibh Éireann
A chúis nach séanaim ás de;
Dá siúlfa, a réalt gan smúid, liom féin,
Ba súgach saor ár sláinte
Gheofá plúr is méad is cnuasach craobh
Sa dún sin Chéin Mhic Cáinte.

Peadar Ó'Dóirnín was born at Rathsgiathach near Forkhill just about a mile and a quarter north of the town of Dundalk in 1704. His father died when he was only nine months old. His mother was of the Established church. When the local clergyman was changed to Drogheda he took Peadar and his mother with him and took good care of his education. He showed an inclination for the study of poetry and the history of Ireland. At an early stage in his life he travelled to Munster and got tuition from a learned Kerryman. From there he went to Connacht, or so we are led to believe, where he studied mathematics and literature and many of the European languages. He was an excellent transcriber of Irish manuscripts.[11]

Because of an agent called Johnson of the Fews who persecuted all the Catholics he came across, Peadar's life was miserable and he spent many years on the run, while depending on friends for refuge. He spent two or three years in the neighbourhood of Forkhill and Mullaghbán and Kilcurry. As his mother was getting old he decided to get back enough of his father's farm to build a house on it. But the relative who held the property which justly belonged to him refused his claim and threatened to inform Johnson. Again he was forced to take refuge with his friends. He spent much of his time on the borders of Armagh where he taught children of farmers in private.

In a short time he taught publicly. He moved to Ash and thence to Kilcurley where he continued to teach. Johnston was called the 'Tory Hunter' and Ó`Dóirnín could never be persuaded to sing his praises. After his mother's death Peadar moved to a little village called Mecog, at Ballyberwick. He made friends with Colman More and taught his children at night-time. The chief reason he stayed there was that he fell in love with Rose Ó'Doirnín, known as 'Sweet little Rose with the coal-black hair'. She was the sister of Mrs Colman. He married her and they were both very happy living on part of his brother-in law's land. Rose did not live long. After her death Peadar moved on. Before he did this he composed a poem called *Eachtra an Ghearain Bháin* for an old horse of Colman's which he was obliged to ride on a journey.

He moved to Drogheda and stayed for quite a while. When he returned to Dundalk he composed Madge Thompson and Seamus Mhac Moineanta. Johnson sent him word one day that he could keep a school in any place he chose. Peadar started to teach in the neighbourhood of Lochross. He still concealed himself as he was afraid that Johnson's murderers might capture him. Johnson was always afraid of Peadar's satire. To make sure he would have all on his side he (Johnson) invited all the Catholic clergy of his neighbourhood to a feast at the top of Sliabh Gullion. Peadar went also, knowing that he was among friends.

After the feast the bards were called upon to show their skills. His friends persuaded him to compose a song for Johnson which he did. Later Peadar was instrumental in saving Johnson's life. In return Johnson promised him protection. This was how Peadar ventured to appear in public and to teach near Forkhill. It was here he composed his only poem in English- *The Independent Man.*

> Here's a health to all those that at liberty go
> That travel the road without a command
> That drink and that sport, that sit in their clothes
> Whilst taking repose with a glass in their hand.
> I'm one of the sort, the track of their sole,
> I love it by jove, while e'er I stand,
> I'll keep my own 'Vote' I'll give it to none
> I value no more a Parliament Man.
> For kings or their guards I care not a straw
> No colour at all shall make me stand,
> To Dukes or to Lords or to Ladys at ball
> I never will crawl with cap in my hand.
>
> A Whig or a Tory, High Church or Low Church,
> Protestant, Roman, Quaker or Clan
> Shall n'er control me to any other notion
> Bur the same motive I have in hand.
> I'll travel the road, I'll meddle with none,
> I'll let them alone by sea and by land,
> For Providence store me want of their board,
> I'm covered with clothes and that's my demand.

The gentry were his friends and in particular Mr. Brownlow of Lurgan. It was while Brownlow was electioneering that Peadar composed the above poem.

On the morning of the 3 April 1769 in his school in Forkhill, he felt himself getting drowsy and while the children were out playing in the fields he lay on the bench and died shortly afterwards. News spread and his neighbours and friends carried him to the mills of Rathbainne, where he was waked according to the custom of the old Irish. He was interred in his mother's grave. Gentry and peasantry from Louth, Armagh, and Monaghan attended his funeral. All the neighbouring musicians were there. The harp resounded to the slow note of sorrow of the mourners. The dirge- women (Caoiners) were there and Art McCúmhaigh sang the elegy on the grave of his friend. The following is an English translation.

On Yellow Fort Hill, meditating one day in the Spring
I heard the nine Muses lament while the cuckoos did sing
Parmassus, near Troy, was annoyed with sorrow and care,
And the fairy mounds around abounded with grief and despair.

Luna, and Phoebus were eclipsed and lost their light,
Mars and bright Venus with Mercury aloft took to flight
And Saturn great was reading the fate of mankind,
And Jupiter sage in a rage the heavens resigned.

One thousand, seven hundred and sixty nine to a day
Three months being expired, the age of Our Lord it is said'
On the 5th day of April the eloquent bard was entombed
Ó'Dóirnín the great, unequalled for verses and poems.
Oh! My consolation and faithful companions flown
Who never to do abase act to any was known
But now, with affection, historians his value proclaim
As his verses flowed freely as nectar from Helicon's stream.

Ovid was famed for framing practical lays
And Horace the great, who wrote with such power and ease,
O'Dóirnín had favoured great Virgil, the sweet and sublime
And Homer from Greece, whose volumes set forth in his time.

Hybernia the fair in despair and sorrow complains,
And we hear the lament that is sent all over the plains
But he's fled it is said from that lovely green Isle in the West
To the regions where legions of Irish are happy and blessed.

Modern Times

During the 1960s and 70s the name of Mark's Bar (proprietors: Mark and Maeve McLoughlin) in Dundalk was legendary among the followers of traditional music every where. It was without a doubt one of the most notable pubs of its day. Resident musician Peter Mc Ardle who hailed from Tallanstown, a few miles outside Dundalk, a fiddler of extraordinary talent, became part of the establishment. He was looked upon as the "Bard". He was an authority on the South Armagh and Louth tradition. I could not name all the young musicians he helped. Many have made international names for themselves. He lived on the premises and there was joy in the eyes of all who met and knew him. Mark's Bar was a pub with character. Celtic murals covered the ceilings and walls and the most wonderful antiques peeped down on you from corners and shelves. All kinds of characters met here, and time flew as the music played non-stop. I can only remember some of the visitors such as Leslie Bingham and his wife and family. Leslie was an expert on the Uilleann pipes. His daughter Tara and Dermy Diamond had their wedding reception there. Dan Dowd was a frequent visitor from Dublin as was Barry Ward from Swords. The Sands family never failed to call. Tommy's songs regaled us all and their music was special. Tommy composed and recorded a song he called "Peter on The Fiddle". Tommy's father and mother had an open house on the Ryan Road for all, and he said Mark and Maeve McLoughlin were like a father and mother to all the rambling musicians of Ireland and beyond. Tommy played the guitar and sang. Ann was a lovely girl, a good singer and played the bodhran. Colm sang, played the fiddle, viola, bass, harmonium and guitar. Ben played piano and mandolin and Dino who was later killed in Germany played mandolin and whistle and sang.

It was sad when Peter died and we all played traditional music in the church and at the grave. Fergal McAulliffe led the cortege as the lone piper playing 'The Ulster Outcry.' Dan Healy on the concert flute, Gerry McCartney on banjo, Paddy Tyrrell on flute, Seán Garvey on accordion and Des Wilkinson on flute were there. Len Graham, Seán Cochrane, Joe Stewart, Finbar Boyle and so many more musicians came in droves from the Glens of Antrim. Little did any of us know that Dino Sands would be joining Peter in that joyous place we all hope to see some day. And we repeated the playing at his burial as the tears streamed down and our hearts broke with sorrow.

The O'Hanlons of Mullaghbán were frequent visitors to Mark's Bar. Dinny O'Brien and his musical family were frequent callers. Alas there is no music there any more. Mark and Maeve moved on in 1979 and left a gap never to be filled. But we all have those wonderful memories.

APPENDIX I
Collectors and Musicians

Henry Morris -Énrí Ó' Muirgheasa

Henry was born in Coolfure, in the county of Monaghan, Barony of Farney 1873. He went to school in Lisdoonan in 1883. He was appointed monitor in 1888. He later became an authority on ancient monuments in Monaghan, Louth, Donegal, Sligo and Leitrim. He became interested in "caint na ndaoine" (the dialect of the people). He joined the Gaelic League, and taught in two places - Coranure and Laragh. He was the driving force behind the spread of the Gaelic League in Monaghan.

In 1901 he got a teaching job in St. Malachy's, in Dundalk where he was one of the founders of the Louth Archaeological Society in 1904. He married Ms Alice Reilly who was interested in Archaeology and was a keen Harpist. All this time he was writing, "Sean-Fhocla Uladh" and "Dunbo agus scéalta eile". Tragedy hit the family and he lost his son and his wife in the same year 1908. He remarried in 1912.

In 1915 he published "Céad de Cheoltaibh Uladh" and in 1916 he published "Amhráin Airt Mhic Cubhtaigh". He was sent to Skerries as school inspector and was later transferred to Sligo. In the introduction to "Céad de Ceoltaibh Ulaidh" Henry Morris tells us that the collection of the popular Irish songs of the people had already been fairly well done in Munster, and Connacht; but Ulster had been a neglected province. Seeing this he began a collection of the scattered remnants of Ulster literature and he was lucky to get a number of Irish MSS., belonging to Matthew Moore Graham of Dundalk. "Céad de Ceoltaibh Uladh" is the first volume of modern Irish Ulster poetry ever published.

Morris' research revealed that a Bardic Convention was held in Dundalk as late as 1827. Irish songs were composed and written into MSS., in Louth, Armagh and Cavan as late as 1860 and the copying of MSS was continued until 1900. Henry Morris died in 1945.

Eugene O'Curry, John O'Donovan and George Petrie

A most farseeing man, Eugene O'Curry 's aim in life was to ensure that the Ireland of the future should be bound with the Ireland of the past. This ideal he had before him throughout his life. He was born at Dunaha West, about three miles south of Kilkee in 1794. His father was Eoghan Mór. He had a vast traditional knowledge of Irish Literature. The Irish language and music was an important part of their life during the 19th century. The traditional love of learning and the copying of Irish Manuscripts was extensively carried on. Eugene's father was an expert storyteller and seanchaí. Times were bad. Poverty had set in, in many places. Teaching was not easy and he tells us at one stage the furniture was stolen from the school.

Around 1824 he worked as a labourer on the construction of the new bridge across the Shannon. In the early thirties the publishing firm of Hodges Smith (now Hodge Figgis) received a commission to purchase Irish manuscripts for the Royal Irish Academy. They were introduced to O'Curry who joined the Ordinance Survey staff in 1835. O'Curry's great work of this time can never be forgotten. It must be mentioned that Dublin in those years led a life apart from the rest of Ireland. The Royal Irish Academy was founded in 1795, for the study of polite literature and antiquities. Then, the three great men O' Donovan, O'Curry and George Petrie brought about a complete change.

John O'Donovan was born at Atateenmore Co. Kilkenny in 1809. He was educated in Dublin and in 1829, he was appointed to a post in the Ordinance Survey of Ireland. He visited every part of Ireland and made notes of many volumes which are preserved in the Royal Irish Academy. He wrote many articles on Irish topography, and history. In 1836, he commenced compiling the catalogue of the Irish Manuscripts in the library in Trinity. Then he devoted himself to preparing an edition of the "Annals of the Four Masters". The R.I.A. presented him with it's highest distinction - the gold Cunningham Medal"

The R.I.A. provided a place for the housing of historic manuscripts. In 1827 George Petrie (1790-1866) became a member and found the material scattered all over the house. In 1829 he became a member if the Council. It was at this time Mr. Smith of Hodges Figgis, went to Limerick and met Eugene Curry. When John O'Donovan and O'Curry joined the R.I.A. the trio founded and placed Irish Studies and linguistics on a firm and scientific basis.

In 1824, the House of Commons ordered a survey and valuation of the land. The Department of Geography, History, and Antiquities was entrusted to Petrie and he quickly brought O' Curry and O'Donovan with him. The outdoor work was done by O'Donovan. O'Curry remained in Dublin picking out illustrative extracts from ancient manuscripts. These three scholars worked on the survey until 1842 and 193 volumes were deposited in the R.I.A.

At the height of their achievements the grant to the Topographical and History Departments was withdrawn and they were left to fend for themselves. This was a political move. Ireland was as yet part of the British Empire. The work of these scholars gave inspiration to the Young Irelanders. The Nation paper was founded by Thomas Davis and a number of scholarly societies were founded; The Irish Archaeological Society in 1840, The Celtic Society, 1845 and The Ossianic Society in 1854. Gradually the public became aware of the of the scholarly work being carried out. 'The Nation' helped to publish material from the ancient manuscripts compiled by O'Donovan and O'Curry. It was at this time O'Donovan with the help of O'Curry translated *The Annals of the Four Masters.*

In 1842 O'Curry was employed to compile a descriptive catalogue of their Manuscripts. They also worked on "Leabhar Breac", "Leabhar na gCeart", and the "Book of Lecan". O'Curry went to London in 1849. He came across the "Tripartite Life of St. Patrick" and catalogued 519 Irish Folios in the British Museum. These men had so little to live on that they contemplated emigration. And then the Brehon Law Commission was set up in 1852 and the three men were employed with a good salary.

When the Catholic University was established O'Curry was asked by Cardinal Newman to take the chair of Irish History and Archaelogy. He continued to edit for the Celtic Society. He wrote *Manners and Customs of the ancient Irish.*

In his lecture on "Music and Musical Instruments in Erin" he said, *In no country in Europe, at least I believe so, is the antiquity and influence of the harp thrown so far back into the dark regions of history, as in Erin.* Our traditions are more distinct than those of the Greeks, for they give time and place name, and occasion.

His famous lectures in the Catholic University were published in two great volumes, as "Lectures on the Manuscript Material of Irish History". This super human work was too much for him and he died of a heart attack in 1862 after he delivered his final lecture. Six months later John O'Donovan died.

Denis Hempson: The harper who lived to 112 years

Denis Hempson was born in the townland of Craigmore, near Garvagh, Co. Derry in 1695. He became blind at three from smallpox. At twelve he began to study the harp with the assistance of Bridget O' Cathán. In those days women as well as men were taught the harp. Denis later was helped by three Connacht harpers, Loughlin Fanning, Patrick O'Connor and John C. Gallagher. At the age of eighteen he began to play for a living. He spent six months in the house of George Canning at Garvagh. He travelled widely throughout Ireland and in Scotland for ten years. Francis O'Neill says "his conversation was as entertaining as his music was entrancing".

He was fifty years old when he returned to Scotland, in 1745 where he was called upon to play for "Bonnie Prince Charlie", the Pretender. He had been in Carolan's company when he was a youth, but never took pleasure in playing his compositions. He pre-ferred the ancient airs like, the *Coulin, Eileen a Rún* and the *Dawning of the Day.* He was a gay bachelor until the age of eighty six when he married a lady at Magilligan. They had a daughter with whom he spent the last years of his life.

By the end of the eighteenth century, the Irish harp was on the verge of extinction and efforts were made to revive Irish music. The result was the first ever Harp Festival in Belfast in 1792. Among those who attended were Arthur O'Neill, aged 58, Daniel Black, 75, Charles Byrne, 80, Hugh Higgins, 47, William Carr, 15, Rose Mooney, 52 and James Duncan, 45. Denis Hempson who the oldest musician there. It was with great difficulty Bunting coaxed tunes from him. Hempson died in 1807. He had lived in three centuries and played the harp for 100 years.

James Hardiman

James Hardiman, author of *Irish Minstrelsy* was born in Westport in 1782 as far as we can gather. He was a contemporary of John O'Donovan, Eugene O'Curry, George Petrie and James Henthorn Todd. In 1815, Hardiman was appointed sub-commissioner in the Patent Rolls office. He helped Thomas Davis when he started the Young Irelanders and he was a friend James Clarence Mangan.

James Hardiman's father came from Meath just a few miles from where O'Carolan was born. In 1813, he rented a house at 36, Wellington St. He and his wife and his mother lived here. Marcella Hall was his mother's name and she came from outside Castlebar. Hardiman studied law, and became an attorney in 1815. He was not short of wealth, and in 1818 he bought land in the barony of Carra in Mayo for £1000. Two years before that his mother left him a small farm the same barony. By this time he had about two hundred acres which he rented out for £800 per year.

While working for the Commission he took a special interest in the history and culture of Ireland. He contributed translations and notes on ancient deeds and land to the Royal Irish Academy. In 1820 he published *The History of the Town and County of Galway*. He did this at his own expense. Following the death of George 1V in 1830, the Commission of Public Records was abolished and Hardiman lost his job as sub-commissioner. He moved to Galway in 1830.

He bought a new house "Taylor's Hill" with eight acres of land.
He is without a doubt responsible for the preservation of the works of Raftery, MacSweeney and Riocard Bairéad. He wrote down the poems of O'Carolan and published them in *Irish Minstrelsy*. He also published seventeenth and eighteenth century poems. O'Donovan was his scribe. His published books and articles were - *A Statute Passed at a Parliament* held at Kilkenny in 1376 and *A Topographical Description of West or H-Iar Connaught* written by Roderick O'Flaherty in the seventeenth century and edited by Hardiman in 1846.
Hardiman was a major figure in the history of Irish literature. He was highly competent as an archivist and as a lawyer. He was generous and helpful during the famine

years to the starving. He made donations of books to local libraries and gave ten acres of his own land to the Franciscans at Errew for a school. He has made a remarkable contribution to his country by his collection and preservation of ancient material. He was one of the members of the first committee who set up the Irish Archaeological Society. Dr.Todd was appointed the first secretary in 1840 and Hardiman was invited by Todd to be a member of the society. In Galway, he was appointed official lawyer to the City Commissioners. He was also, a member of the Galway Royal Institute. Both Hardiman and O'Donovan were given posts in the Universities of Galway and Belfast. Hardiman chose the Librarianship of U.C.G. and today the library is called after him. He died in 1855.

Thomas Furlong

Thomas Furlong was born in Co. Wexford. His father was a respectable farmer and Thomas was born at Scarawalsh, a romantic part of the country midway between Ferns and Eniscorthy. He had a good education and was apprenticed to a respectable trader in Dublin. He always had a passion for poetry and when his employer died he composed a poem called *The Burial*.

'Oh! If the atheist's words were true,
If those we seek to save,
Sink - and in sinking from our view
Are lost beyond the grave!
If life thus closed - how dark and drear
Would this bewildered earth appear,
Scarce worth the dust it gave .
A tract of black sepulchral gloom
One yawning ever-opening tomb.

Blest be that strain of high belief
More heaven - like, more sublime,
Which says, that souls that part in grief,
Part only for a time!
That far beyond this speck of pain
Far o'er the gloomy grave's domain
There spreads a brighter clime
Where care and toil, and trouble o'er
Friends meet, and meeting, weep no more.

He got employment from Mr. Jamieson the well-known distiller in Dublin. It has been said that Jamieson wept like a child the day of his funeral. Furlong has a few poems to his credit and he translated many poems especially those collected by James Hardiman. He printed a few verses which he called "Lines written in a blank page of Lady Morgan's *Italy*". Lady Morgan responded as follows.

"Your poem written in the blank page of 'Italy' has been read and admired by persons of more judgement than her whom it must naturally most interest. Feeling and writing as you do I trust you will not neglect 'the goods the good God provides ' I shall always be happy to hear of your literary exertions, without entertaining a doubt of their success".

29th March 1822, Kildare Street.
I am, etc.
Sydney Morgan

He contributed to many magazines in London and Dublin, mostly parodies. His health started to decline, and after a short confinement to his bed, he died on the 25th July 1827. He was just thirty-three years of age. He was buried in the churchyard of Drumcondra, in Dublin. Over his grave, which lies near that of Grosse, his friends erected a handsome monument, which bears the inscription:

To the memory of
Thomas Furlong, Esq.
In whom the purest principles of
Patriotism and Honour
Were combined with Superior Poetical Genius
This Memorial of Friendship
Is erected by those who valued and admired
His various Talents, Public Integrity And Private Worth.
He died 25th July 1827. Aged 33 years.
May He rest In Peace.

The following poem was written a few days before his death.

The Spirit of Irish Song

Lov'd land of the Bards and Saints! To me
There's nought so dear as thy minstrelsy;
Bright is Nature in every dress,
Rich in unborrow'd loveliness;
Winning is every shape she wears,
Winning she is in thine own sweet airs;
What to the spirit more cheering can be
Than the lay whose ling'ring notes recall
The thoughts of the holy -the fair- the free
Belov'd in life or deplor'd their fall?
Fling, Fling the forms of art aside,
Dull is the earth that these forms enthral;
Let the simple songs of our sires be tried
They go to the heart -and the heart is all.
Give me the full responsive sigh,
The glowing cheek and the moisten'd eye;
Let these the minstrel's might attest,
And the vain and idle - may share the rest.

APPENDIX 2
Arthur Darley and the Mummers Tunes

Arthur Darley, who died in 1929 was a native of Dun Laoghaire. He was president of the Irish Music Club and one of the founders of the Feis Ceoil Association. He collected airs from a cross section of singers, musicians and whistlers. It is interesting to note that some of these tunes are associated with mumming, a form of drama which originated in the Middle Ages. The word mumming is Teutonic in origin and means mask. The mumming tradition which flourished in England from the late fourteenth century became popular in Ireland from the time of Henry VIII. The Punch and Judy shows are a form of mumming.

Nowadays in Ireland mumming is a tradition mostly associated with Wexford, Swords and Armagh. The *Mummers' March* came from Patrick Whelan and it is No.68 in Darley's book. Darley calls it *Drockety's March*. It was played on the flute by John Ferguson (locally known as 'Vargus'), a farm labourer from Rathangan, Co. Wexford. It was performed in Wexford every winter. Drockety is a corruption of Draoicht, meaning enchantment or magic. John Ferguson also played the *Mummers Jig* and the *Duncormick Jig*.   Other mumming tunes include the *Mad Cap, O'Donovan's Reel, O'Dwyer's Hornpipe, The Red Moon Jig and Vargus' Jig*.

THE MUMMERS' JIG AND REEL

DUNCORMICK MUMMERS' JIG

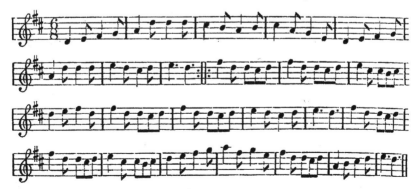

A MUMMERS' REEL *Taken down from Dan Healy*

68 DROCKETTY'S MARCH

REFERENCES

Chapter 1:
1. Folklore from my late father, J. McDonnell of Tobracken.
2. Photo of Roscommon men taken probably after Mass.
3. Eating on the bog on a sunny day.
4. Tim Kenny's shop was sold long ago. It is now a supermarket.
5. Bradshaw, Harry. Michael Coleman 1891-1945. (1991). Vive Voce.
6. Breathnach, Brendán. Folk Music and dances of Ireland. Mercier Press, Dublin and Cork (1971).
7. Giblin, P.J. Collection of Traditional Irish Folk Music for the Violin. Germany (1828).
8. Towey, Brother John F.S.C. Ph.D. Irish De La Salle Brothers in Christian Education. Folens, Dublin. (1980).
9. Photograph of young Walkinstown musicians playing at a concert in Moran's Hotel, Dublin (1964).

Chapter 2
1. Grattan Flood, W.H. A History of Irish Music (1905). Re-issued in 1970.
2. Joyce, W.P. A Social History of Ancient Ireland. Longmans, Green, and Co., Dublin. M.H. Gill & Son (1910).
3. Grattan Flood, W.H. A History of Irish Music (1905). Re-issued in 1970.
4. Ibid.
5. O'Connor, Charles. Memories of Life and Writings of the late Charles O'Connor of Belanagare Esq. M.R.I.A. (1797) J Mehain NO49 Essex St., Dublin.
6. Grattan Flood, W.H. A History of Irish Music (1905). Re-issued in 1970.
7. McDonagh J.C. Vol I/XXXVII. County Sligo Reference Library.
8. O'Neill, Francis. Irish Minstrels and Musicians.
9. Traditional Irish Music Archives, 63 Merrion Square, Dublin.
10. O'Neill, Francis. Irish Minstrels and Musicians.
11. Millington Fox, Charlotte. Annals of the Irish Harpers. J. Murray, London.
12. O'Laoghaire, An tAthair Peadar. Sgothbhualadh. Brún agus O'Nualláin, Dublin.

Chapter 3
1. Cooper Walker, Joseph. Historical Memoirs of the Irish Bards. T. Payne and Son, London.
2. O'Tuama, Seán. Caoineadh Airt Uí Laoghaire. Baile Atha Cliath.
3. Cooper Walker, Joseph. Historical Memoirs of the Irish Bards. T. Payne and Son, London.
4. O'Sullivan, Donal. Carolan: The Life ,Times and Music of an Irish Harper. Routledge and Kegan Paul Ltd., London (1958)
5. Royal Irish Academy. MS. 24125, ff. 25-30; MS. 24131, ff. 202-12.
6. Campbell, Mary. Autobiography, Diaries and Correspondence of Lady Morgan. The Life and Times of Sydney Owenson vols 1 &2. London.
7. Ó'Céirín, Kit and Cyril. Women of Ireland. Tír Eolas, Galway.
8. O'Neill Maire. From Parnell to DeValera. Biography of Jenny Wyse-Power. Blackwater Press (1991).

Chapter 4

1. Hardiman, James Irish Ministrelsy Vols I & 2, London (1831).
2. Ó Coighligh, Ciarán. Raiftéirí, Amhráin agus Dánta. Baile Atha Cliath. (1987).
3. Gibbons, Dr. Hugh. Oral Information on Dr. Hyde and Kilmactranny.
4. ibid.
5. De híde, Dubhghlas. Amhráin Grádh Chúige Chonnacht.
6. Uí Choisdealbha, Eibhlín. Amhráin Mhuighe Seóla. London (1918)
7. De híde, Dubhghlas. Amhráin agus Dánta an Reachtabhraigh. (1933).
8. Uí Choisdealbha, Eibhlín. Amhráin Mhuighe Seóla. London (1918)

Chapter 5

1 O'Sullivan, Donal. Carolan: The Life ,Times and Music of an Irish Harper. Routledge and Kegan Paul Ltd., London (1958).
2 Grattan Flood, W.H. A History of Irish Music (1905). Re-issued in 1970.
3 O'Sullivan, Donal. Carolan: The Life ,Times and Music of an Irish Harper. Routledge and Kegan Paul Ltd., London (1958).
4 McDonagh. J.C. Vol I-XXX VII, Reference Library, Sligo.
5 O'Sullivan, Donal. The Memoirs of Arthur O'Neill in Carolan: The Life ,Times and Music of an Irish Harper Routledge and Kegan Paul Ltd., London (1958).
6 O'Connor, Charles. Memories of Life and Writings of the late Charles O'Connor of Belanagare Esq. M.R.I.A. (1797) J Mehain No.49 Essex St., Dublin.
7. Hardiman, James Irish Ministrelsy Vols I & 2, London (1831).

Chapter 6

1. Kilgallon, Tadhg, History of Sligo, Kilgallon and Son Ltd.Sligo (1926)
2. Wood-Martin, Colonel William Gregory, History of Sligo.
3. O'Dowd, Mary : Power, Politics & and Land, Early Modern Sligo. (1568-1688) Institute of Irish Studies, Queen's University, Belfast.
4. O'Brien, Conor Cruise: The Great Melody, A thematic biography of Edmund Burke. Great Britian , by Sinclair-Stephenson , London. (1992)
5. Crofton, Henry. Crofton Memoirs. Yorkshire Printing Company. (1911)
6. O'Sullivan, Donal. The Life Times and Music of an Irish Harper. Routledge and Kegan Paul Ltd., London (1958).
7. Perceval, Serena Temple House, Ballymote. Information on the history of Temple House Co. Sligo.
8. Crofton, Henry. Crofton Memoirs. Yorkshire Printing Company. (1911)
9. O'Muraíle, Nollaig. The Celebrated Antiquary – Dubhaltach Mac Fhirbhisigh An Sagart, Maynooth. (1996)
10. O'Dowd, Mary: Power Politics and Land, Early Modern Sligo.1568-1668
11. O'Muraíle, Nollaig:The Celebrated Antiquary - Dubhaltach Mac Fhirbhisigh. An Sagart Maynooth. (1996)

12. O'Sullivan, Donal: . Carolan: The Life ,Times and Music of an Irish Harper.
13. ibid
14. O'Dowd, Mary; Power Politics and Land 1568-1688.
15. Hardiman, James : Irish Minstrelsy, Vol 1 & 2.
16. O'Dowd, Mary: Power Politics and Land, Early Modern Sligo 1568-1688.
17. Aikenhead Sr.Mary, Her Life, Her Work & Her Friends. Published, Dublin 1879
18. Mac Dermot, Dermot; Mac Dermot of Moylurg, The Story of a Connacht Family. Mac Dermot Clann Association, Naas, Co. Kildare.

Chapter 7

1 Music Collected by Dan Healy from Art McMorrow in Collooney, Co. Sligo.
2 Fearghal O'Gadhra (Reel) written by Ciarán O' Reilly.
3 O'Dowd, Mary: Power Politics and Land – Early Modern Ireland.
4 O'Neill, Captain Francis: The Dance Music of Ireland. Edited by Selena O'Neill, Chicago.
5 Breathnach, Brendán. ed. Ceol – A Journal of Irish Music 1965, page 13 –
The Man & His Music.
6 McHugh, Patrick, Memories of Monasteraden, Growing up in the Thirties. Edited by Rev. Thomas Mulligan, Cloonloo, Monasteraden, Barony of Coolavin, Co. Sligo.
7 Ibid
8 Information and photos given by John O'Gara of Killavil.

Chapter 8

1 Ó Catháin Séamus, Béaloideas Éireann. The Living Landscape, Killgalligan, Erris, Co. Mayo.
2 Scéalta Chois Cladaigh, told by John Henry Kilgalligan , Maigh Eo
3 Nolan, Rita :Within the Mullett, Galway.
4 Ibid
5 Ibid
6 Four Centuries of Irish Music –Edited by Brian Boydell, British Broadcasting Corporation London.
7 Millington Fox, Charlotte: Annals of the Irish Harpers. John Murray Abbeyrmarle St. W. London.(1911).
8 Ibid
9 ibid
10 Mac Giolla Fhínnan, Brian,: Journal of the Armagh Historical Society Vol. 15. No.2
11 Gadelica :Ed.Tómás Ó Raghallaigh. A journal of Modern Irish Studies. Hodge Figgis & Co. Dublin 1912
12 Trotter, John B.Esq. Walks Through Ireland 1812,1813, 1817. Sir Richard Phillips & Co. BrideCourt, Bridge St Gaelic Journal No 57 Page 137.
13 Ó. Dúilearga, Séamus, Bealoideas, IML X Abhráin Ó Iorrais.
14 Ó Máille, Micheál agus Tomás Ámhráin Chlainne Gael.
15 Amhráin Ghaeilge an Iarthair.Collected by Mícheál ÓTiománaidhe.

16 Ibid.

17 Ibid.

18 Gaelic Songs of the West   - Seamas Cosgar

19 Amhráin Ghaeilge an Iarthair , Micheál Ó Tiománaidhe.

20 Targaireacht Bhriain Ruaidh Uí Chearbháin Red Brian's Prophecy Part 1 Collected by Michael Timony1906 Padhraig Daeid, An File Leat.46.

21 West or h-Iar Connaught 1684 By Roderick O'Flaherty with notes by James Hardiman.

22 O'Conaire. Brendán,- The Songs of Connacht.

23 Cooper Walker, Joseph, Memoirs of the Irish Bards.

Chapter 9

1. O'Sullivan, Donal. Carolan, the Life Times and Music of an Irish Harper.

2. Ibid

3. Tempo Manor Estate History

4. Morris, Henry: The Modern Irish Poets of Oriel Breffni, and Meath. Co. Louth. Archaelogical Society. (1906)

5. Morris, Henry: The Modern Irish Poets of Oriel Breffni, and Meath. Co. Louth. Archaelogical Society. (1906) Dundalk Feis 1904

6. Morris, Henry, Co Louth Archaelogical Society 1904. (list of Poets)

7. Bennett, Art, Welcome to Mac Cuarta. Louth Archaelogical Journal 1904.

8. Bennett, Art, Carolaniana. Louth Archaelogical Journal 1911.

9. Ó' Doibhlin, Crónán, Archive Co-ordinator, Tí Chulainn, An Mullach Bán, an tÍur, Observations on Padraig Mac Alindon. 1999.

10. Ó'Máille, Tomás M.A. PhD. Amhráin Chearbhalláin. The Irish Text Society 20 Hanover Square London.

11. Moore Graham, Matthew. (Scribe)The Bardic Remains of Co. Louth, Vol.1 from the Irish of O Dóirnín. Taken from the Contents of MSS. (1831) in possession of Henry Morris.

INDEX